Death or Deliverance

By Susan E. Hilliard

Illustrated by Ned O.

STANDARD PUBLISHING

Cincinnati, Ohio   24-03988

Library of Congress Cataloging-in-Publication Data

Hilliard, Susan E.
    Death or deliverance / by Susan E. Hilliard.
        p.   cm. — (Decide your own adventure)
    Summary: The reader's decisions control visits to several
Biblical prophets, including Jonah, Ezekiel, and Nahum.
    ISBN 0-87403-728-X
    1. Prophets—Biography—Juvenile literature. 2. Bible.
O.T. Prophets—Biography—Juvenile literature. 3. Plot-
your-own stories. 4. Bible. O.T.—Prophecies—Juvenile lit-
erature.   [1. Prophets.   2. Bible stories—O.T.—   3.
Plot-your-own-stories.] I. Title. II. Series: Hilliard, Susan E.
Decide your own adventure.
BS1198.H541990
224'.09505—dc20   90-33965
                                                       CIP
Edited by Theresa C. Hayes   AC

Scripture quoted is from the *Holy Bible, New International
Version.* Copyright © 1973, 1978, International Bible Society. Used by permission of Zondervan Bible Publishers and
the International Bible Society.

Attention, Reader!

You cannot read this book as you would any other. You are embarking upon a very special quest for truth. In this journey, you will travel in a chariot of fire as you search for the answers to your quest. During your travel you will sometimes be allowed to choose between alternate times and events. When you decide where you want to go, the chariot will take you swiftly to your destination.

When you find the chariot, look for two scrolls of parchment in it. One parchment is a vital archive of historical facts that can aid you in making the right choice at the proper time. A separate, smaller scroll will contain the object of your quest.

And now, begin the adventure!

The Chariot

A chariot of fire stands before you. The chariot itself seems solid enough, although it appears to be completely in flames. Your heart thudding with excitement, you step closer and notice that the fire is not hot, only pleasantly warm. Through the shimmering flames you see a beautiful horse hitched to the chariot, standing patiently. The animal seems so serene that you find your heart is not hammering quite so violently, and you hesitantly step into the chariot. Nothing happens. You are surrounded by flames, yet nothing is burning. You step farther into the chariot, and notice a plain wooden box on the floor. Upon the box is written, "Rules for Travel." You open the box.

On the inside of the lid, you read....

Rules for Travel

You must follow these rules on your journey. If you do not, the chariot will return you to the present, and you will never be able to complete your quest.

I. You may not change history in any way — you are only an observer.
II. You may choose only from the alternatives that you are given.
III. You may not bring twentieth-century customs, clothing, or equipment with you. Tell no one you may meet of your journey.
IV. You may not bring any souvenirs of your journey home with you.

You will find that language differences will not be a problem for you. You will automatically think and speak in the language of your host place and time.

Looking into the box, you see a piece of parchment nestled in dark brown folds of thick cloth. Hastily, you pull out the cloth and the parchment flutters to the chariot floor. Glancing at it, you see a rough sketch of a man in a peaked cap. You hold the dark tunic at arms' length, and decide that it will fit.

Quickly you remove your modern clothes and pull on the short-sleeved garment. The long fringe tickles your ankles as you tie a sturdy sash securely around your waist. Only a pair of sandals and a cap remain in the box now, and you swiftly finish dressing. The horse begins pawing the ground impatiently, and your heart begins to hammer in excitement.

Wadding your modern clothes into a ball, you fling them beneath a nearby tree. You drop to your knees, searching for the questions you are to answer on this journey. Your hands grope in the dark corners of the chariot. At last your fingers touch two tightly-rolled cylinders of parchment and you eagerly draw them out. Impatient to begin your journey, you unroll the smaller scroll and read....

The Quest

You are instructed to go to the time of the prophets to find out if all prophets were chosen by God. You are also to discover if their prophecies really came true.

You remember that prophets were sometimes called "watchmen on the wall," and you wonder why. Were all of the prophets' predictions about doom, destruction, and death?

Eagerly you unroll the larger scroll and glance through it. On this scroll, you find written....

Archives

I. God's prophets did more than predict future events. They preached His Word, and were chosen by Him to speak on His behalf.

II. When a prophet predicted doom, he always explained *why* it would happen. No Hebrew could use the excuse that he did not know he was sinning.

III. God takes no pleasure in the death of His creation; the prophets' messages urged the wicked to turn from their ways and *live*.

IV. The prophet Jonah lived during 780-750 B.C. Jesus Christ referred to Jonah as a real, *historical* person.

V. Nineveh was a magnificent city east of the Tigris river. With 1,200 towers, and walls the height of a modern ten-story building, Nineveh would have seemed completely safe from attack. Jonah preached that Nineveh would be overthrown by God in forty days.

VI. The prophet Nahum lived approximately 650 B.C. Very little is known about him, other than his prediction that Nineveh would be totally destroyed.

VII. Tyre was an ancient city by 650 B.C. It was a prosperous port city, known for its sea-going merchants who carried glass and the special dye for which Tyre was famous.

VIII. The city of Petra was the capital of the land of Edom. The buildings were carved from solid rock in the side of the mountain and there was only one entrance—through a narrow canyon.

IX. The prophet Ezekiel lived during the captivity of the Children of Israel in Babylon. Unlike Daniel, who lived in Nebuchadnezzar's palace, Ezekiel lived outside the city.

X. The prophet Isaiah lived in Jerusalem in the eighth century B.C., and prophesied to the Southern Kingdom. Isaiah is called the Messianic Prophet because he foresaw the glory of Christ.

You are sure that you should hang on to this scroll—the information may be helpful. You shove it hurriedly into the sash at your waist, where the folds hide it completely.

You pick up the smooth leather reins, holding them loosely. Your heart begins to hammer in excitement as the steed paws the ground impatiently. You pull the reins taut, and suddenly ....

(At the Beginning)

Gasping and sputtering, you find yourself on the slippery wet planks of a wildly pitching ship. You grab desperately for a secure hold on *something* as the ship keels violently, and you stare in terror at the mountain of grey water bearing down on you. Salt stings your eyes, and you hear the groan of sodden wood protesting as the ship plunges crazily.

"She's breaking up!" cries a sailor near you.

"Quick!" calls an older man, cupping his hands around his mouth to help his voice carry over the shriek of the wind. "Throw the cargo overboard! We must lighten the load!"

Stumbling and falling on the slippery deck, the sailors begin tossing huge baskets over the side of the ship into the sea below. The ship seems to shudder beneath you, and a deafening crack splinters the air.

A violent lurch catches you by surprise, and you find yourself sliding headfirst on your back toward the murky water below. Your arms flail wildly but find nothing to catch onto, and you have one last terrified glimpse of the plunging ship and wind-whipped sail as you slide toward the whirling confusion below you.

A strong hand closes swiftly around your ankle and begins pulling you back. You open your eyes gratefully to see the older man who ordered the cargo thrown overboard. His face is grim as he tugs you to your feet.

"Come with me," he shouts over the wind. "The deck is no place for you now."

You stagger behind him, falling to your knees

every few steps. He disappears down a narrow, dark stairway, and you follow—keeping your arms on the walls to guide your steps down. At the bottom, you enter a shadowy hold. Rows of sailors on low benches strain at oars that fit though holes in the sides of the ship. Weak shafts of light filter into the dark hold from these holes and to your amazement, you see a man curled up and fast asleep in a corner. The older man who saved you strides quickly over to the sleeping form.

"How is it that you are sleeping?" he demands sharply, and his manner leads you to think he must be the captain. He shakes the sleeper's shoulder roughly. "Get up! Call on your god! Perhaps *your* god will see to it that we do not perish!"

The sleeper stands awkwardly as the captain waits, hands on hips. A white-faced sailor approaches nervously, his eyes wide. "Captain!" he quavers. "We cast lots, just now, to learn on whose account this calamity has struck."

"Well?" barks the captain, his brows drawing together in an angry frown.

The frightened sailor looks pleadingly at the man who was asleep. "The lot fell on Jonah, here."

Several other sailors crowd around, eyeing Jonah uneasily. "Tell us, now!" cries one, anguish in his voice. "Why has this calamity struck us? What is your occupation? And where do you come from?"

"What is your country?" calls another. "From what people are you?"

"I am a Hebrew," answers Jonah quietly. "And I fear the Lord God of Heaven who made the sea and the dry land."

The men gasp at yet another deafening crack of wood as the ship's frame shudders.

"How could you do this?" bellows one of the sailors, his eyes desperately afraid. "You told us yourself that you were fleeing from the presence of your god, and look what has happened! What should we do to you that the sea may become calm for us?"

"Pick me up and throw me overboard," Jonah replies. "Then the sea will become calm for you, for I know that on account of me this great storm has come upon you."

The captain shakes his head angrily. "Row!" he shouts, "Row for land!"

The men's glistening backs bend and strain over the oars slicing into the churning sea. The wail of the wind grows louder, and the groan of the ship becomes almost deafening. Quietly, Jonah slips up the stairway that leads to the deck of the ship.

Several men follow him, and you hurry up the steps behind them. A blast of seawater lashes you and the wind tears mercilessly at you. You squint, the salt water painful, staring after Jonah. The sailors' faces are forlorn, as they drop to their knees on the heaving deck.

"We earnestly pray, O Lord," shouts one, his face turned skyward, "Do not let us perish on account of this man's life, and do not hold us responsible for his death; for Thou, O Lord, hast done as Thou hast pleased." Hesitantly they stumble to their feet and approach Jonah. The sailors faces are contorted with grief and fear as they pick him up and pitch him into the furious sea.

Your ears rebel against the instantaneous silence. Black clouds roll away from the ship and mountains of raging water melt into gentle waves. Rosy fingers of dawn light the sailors' faces as you watch awe replace the terror in their expressions. *Poor Jonah!* you think. *What an awful way to die! I guess God was really angry with him.* Suddenly, all is blotted from your sight as you find yourself surrounded by the leaping flames of the chariot of fire.

"It is time for your first choice, my friend," says a quiet voice. A thrill races down your spine as you realize that you are hearing the voice of the magnificent steed.

"You may go to Nineveh, if you wish, to see what happens there. Or you may go almost two-hundred years forward in time to see for yourself the city of Babylon. On which destination shall you decide?"

Thinking carefully about the quest, you take the reins in hands trembling with excitement, and make your decision.

If you decide to go to Nineveh, go to page 21.

If you decide to go forward in time to Babylon, go to page 57.

(You Have Decided to Go Back in Time)

When you notice with surprise that you are still in the chariot, you begin to wish that you had followed the steed's advice. The feeling of hurtling through space makes you uneasy, and you cling more tightly to the cool leather reins. You can see nothing, but suddenly you feel very small and very alone, speeding through time and distance toward an unknown destination. How far back in time will you end up, and where? A knot of fear begins growing in your stomach, and you wish with all your heart that you had made a different decision!

"Do not be afraid, little one," says the steed gently. "You are still—as ever—in His care, you know."

"Is my quest over?" you stammer, wishing you could have found the answers. "Are you taking me home?"

"No—not unless you wish it," replies the voice. "But we cannot escape the results of our decisions. So you must begin again at the beginning."

Relief washes over you that you will be able to finish the quest after all. *Next time*, you decide firmly, *you will choose differently!*

Go to page 11.

(You Have Decided to Find Out How Jonah Survived)

You sputter as a blast of cold seawater breaks against the boulders on which you are standing and smacks you full in the face. The rising sun is shrouded in early-morning fog, and the gray sea mirrors the cloudy sky. You climb carefully down from the rocks to the sandy beach, looking eagerly for Jonah. But the only signs of life in this desolate place are the seagulls overhead.

A white-topped breaker surges onto the sand and your heart beats faster as you see the figure of a man deposited on the sand. *I can't believe he made it to shore!* you think in astonishment as you race toward him. *How long has he been in the sea?*

Slowly, Jonah stands, swaying on weak knees. Slippery tentacles of seaweed are twined around him and he claws at them feebly. You approach him and timidly reach out to help unravel the clinging seaweed. The prophet smiles his thanks to you and suddenly, anger washes over you. *Why did God have to punish him so harshly?* you wonder as you frown. *He could have died out there!*

"What is troubling you, young friend?" Jonah asks softly. "My Lord has worked a wonderous miracle to save me from a grave in the pit of the sea — this is a time for great joy, not anger!"

Your words tumble out. "But, *why*, Jonah? Why did God punish you so harshly?"

The prophet's eyes widen. "Punish me? The Lord is my salvation, youngster! He told me to go Nineveh to preach repentance and instead of obeying Him, I ran the opposite direction! What I *deserved* was death! Instead, the Lord sent a great fish to swallow me, and there, *in the belly of a fish,* the Lord gave me an opportunity to repent! And now! Now He has commanded the fish to deposit me on this shore so that I might have more days of life with which I may serve Him!"

You stare at the prophet in horror. "You were swallowed whole by a *fish*? How awful!"

Jonah throws back his head in a hearty laugh. "It wasn't pleasant, my friend! But compared to the alternative . . ." he shudders. "I calculate that I must have been in the belly of that great fish about three days, and I can assure you that I spent every waking minute in prayer! The Lord has shown His patience once again by giving me back my life."

You frown over this for a moment. "But surely you could be forgiven for being afraid to preach to Nineveh," you argue.

"Afraid?" Jonah laughs again. "I was not afraid! I did not *want* to preach to the Ninevites, because I did not want them to have the opportunity to repent!"

Completely confused, you stare at the prophet. "But, why not?" you falter.

Jonah smiles ruefully. "Nineveh is a bitter enemy of Israel. I wanted to see God destroy them! But I know that God is gracious and compassionate, slow to anger and abundant in lovingkindness—He has certainly demonstrated that here, today, hasn't He?"

You nod, still confused.

"I did not want to preach to Nineveh," Jonah explains, "because I did not want them to repent; I wanted to see them destroyed!"

"Ohhhh," you reply slowly as you begin to understand. "So *that's* why you ran in the opposite direction!"

Jonah frees himself from the last tentacle of seaweed. "Yes, and now the Lord has brought me back to the place where He wanted me—and now I am ready to do His bidding. He *did* punish my rebellion, youngster, but at the same time, He gave me another opportunity to obey Him. And what a punishment!" Jonah smiles ruefully at the memory. "Do you suppose *anyone* will believe that I spent three days and nights in the belly of a fish, and then was vomited out onto a beach?"

You shudder at the thought. "I believe it!" you say emphatically. "And so will anyone who believes that God is all powerful and fully in control of all His creation!"

"Well said, youngster," the prophet replies as he pats you gently on the shoulder. "And now, I'm off to Nineveh!" The leaping flames of the chariot surround you as you and Jonah wave good-bye.

"Now I will take you forward in time to Nineveh, says the steed in its clear, musical voice. "There you will learn the outcome of Jonah's preaching." *Oh good!* you think because you wanted to know what happened there.

Go to page 27.

(You Have Come to Nineveh)

The shimmering flames disappear and you find yourself amidst a crowd on the banks of a slow-moving river. You gasp in astonishment as you lift your eyes across the river and see city walls sweeping skyward. A glint of sun reflecting off metal draws your attention to the very top and you shade your eyes with your forearm as you gaze upward. On the top of the city wall, a chariot moves briskly toward a tower that soars even higher. *Wow!* you think, *Those walls are at least ten stories high and wide enough to drive a chariot on! Just how big is Nineveh?* People are beginning to crowd you now, and you fall into step with them.

The throng carries you with them across a wide stone bridge spanning the river below. Ahead, two huge statues flank massive bronze gates, which are standing open now. You cast a swift glance at the statues, noticing that they are winged bulls with the faces of men.

"Stand aside!" roars a voice, and you and those around you are shoved violently back.

Assyrian soldiers march out of the city gates in columns, their pointed helmets glinting and their tightly-curled and oiled beards glistening in the sun. Spear points bristle in the air as the company marches through the crowd. Mounted archers follow the foot soldiers, and the horses' nostrils flare in excitement. The crowd cheers wildly as, at last, the chariot corps wheel into sight. Each chariot carries four warriors, and their faces are set into grim, menacing masks.

"Bring us back the heads of our enemies!" shrills an old man standing beside you.

The chariot driver closest grins broadly at the old man. "I'll bring you a head for your garden, old man!" he cries.

You shiver in disgust. *Surely they are not serious!* you think. The old man shakes your arm excitedly. "Did you hear that?" he quavers, spittle tracing slowly down his thin grey beard. "He'll bring me a head! No one can stand against the Assyrians!"

You wrench your arm free, pushing through the crowd, not caring *where* you go, as long as you get away from the horrible old man. Jogging down the broad paved street, you notice a ziggurat in the distance rising high above the other city buildings. Without thinking, you turn toward the ziggurat.

After jogging for what feels like hours, you stop, panting, and peer cautiously down an intersecting avenue. At the end of the street, the ziggurat soars above high walls. Palm trees and flowering shrubs grow thickly on each level of the stepped pyramid. Curious, you start down the street to get a closer look at the ziggurat, when the roar of a crowd startles you. Looking around a corner for the source of the sound, you see a huge crowd clustered at the wall surrounding the ziggurat. Excitement surges through you as you trot toward the crowd.

"Yet forty days, and Nineveh will be overthrown!" cries a man.

When you reach the fringe of the crowd, you see white, frightened faces looking anxiously at a man in their midst. He turns, and a thrill races down your spine as you recognize Jonah. *He's alive!* you realize with amazement. *How did he ever get to shore after being thrown overboard?*

"Yet forty days, and Nineveh will be over-thrown!" Jonah repeats solemnly, his eyes sweeping the crowd urgently. Nervously, the people back away, whispering amongst themselves. Jonah moves on, and you hear his message echoing down the street.

You jump as a strong hand falls on your shoulder. "Be quick, youngster!" growls a voice in your ear. "Your legs are younger than mine. The king must know of the prophet's message. Hurry!"

A mighty slap between your shoulder blades sends you running on your way, without ever having a chance to see the man who has sent you. Guessing that the king's palace may be within the stone walls surrounding the ziggurat, you dart through the first opening you find.

Starting across a vast courtyard, you head straight for a massive building opposite. At last, you stand staring up at two shining ebony doors banded with silver and inlaid with ivory. Stone bulls with human faces glare down at you from either side of the double doors, and you shiver as you stand uncertainly in their shadow. From behind you, a group of men approaches the gates, which are suddenly flung open. The men, their faces hidden behind deep cowls, sweep into the palace. Nervously, you decide to follow them.

Your footsteps echo hollowly in the gleaming hallways, and you have a blurred impression of winged bulls carved in alabaster panels on the walls. At last you enter the shadows of a huge

room, where an empty throne stands upon a dais. Quietly, you slip behind a stone pillar.

"The priests are here, O King," whispers a sturdy soldier.

You stare in astonishment, for the man to whom the soldier speaks is sitting on the floor at the foot of the throne. His head is bowed, and he is dressed in a rough black tunic. *Could that be sackcloth he is*

wearing? you wonder. Slowly, the man raises his head. The cowled men have prostrated themselves on the floor before him, and his voice is so low you have to strain to hear it.

"In Nineveh, by the decree of the king and his nobles," the king says solemnly, "Do not let man, beast, herd, or flock taste a thing. Do not let them eat or drink water."

You glance sharply at the soldier who guards the king and see that his eyes are wide and fearful. The priests watch their king intently, their eyes glittering in the deep shadows of their cowls.

"Let both man and beast be covered with sackcloth, and let men call on God earnestly that each may turn from his wicked way and from the violence which is in his hands," continues the king, his voice now gathering strength. "Who knows, God may turn and relent, and withdraw His burning anger so that we shall not perish."

The king must have already heard Jonah's message, you realize, *and he has decided to repent.*

Shimmering flames engulf you. "Behold the king of Nineveh," chimes the musical voice of the steed. "Now you must make a decision. I may take you a few days forward in time, if you choose to see what happens in Nineveh. Or I may take you to a beach on the Mediterranean find out how Jonah's life was saved. Which will you decide?"

Well, it would be interesting to see what happens to Nineveh, you think, *but how did Jonah survive?* Choosing carefully, you take the reins in your hands and pull them taut.

If you decide to go a few days forward in time, go to page 27.

If you decide to find out how Jonah survived, go to page 18.

(You Have Decided to Go a Few Days Forward in Nineveh)

Sunbeams slant down through a window cut high in the stone wall at your back, pointing fingers of light at a row of stalls. Dust dances lazily in the shafts of sunlight and the scent of hay tickles your nose. A warm breath blows on the back of your neck, and a soft whinney sounds in your ear. You turn to discover a beautiful chestnut horse nuzzling you hopefully. The animal is covered in rough, black cloth, and as you peer through the early-morning light at the other horses in their stalls, you see that *all* are covered in the same black material. You slip quickly out of the stall, carefully closing and latching the wooden gate behind you.

"You there!" shouts a voice. "You're not feeding or watering the animals, are you?"

Whirling around, you see a stout older man limping toward you furiously. He, too, is wearing a rough, scratchy-looking tunic of black. The sun makes a halo of his grizzled grey hair, and his dark eyes sparkle angrily as he faces you in the stables.

"No, I didn't feed or water them," you protest firmly.

Sighing, his lined face relaxes into a rueful smile." I'm sorry, youngster," he says gently, "I didn't mean to snap at you. But it is a matter of life and death, you know!"

The horses are moving impatiently in their stalls now, their whinnies eager as they eye the man expectantly.

"No, no, my beauties," the man says firmly. "No food or water for you, by order of the king of Nineveh. You'll live, my great beasts, you'll live!"

"Why did the king give such an order?" you ask.

The man turns swiftly to you, and gasps. "You are not wearing sackcloth—this will never do!" He limps quickly to an empty stall, removing a blanket of black cloth. Whipping a small knife from the sash of his tunic, he hastily cuts a hole in the fabric, and then flings the blanket over your head, poncho-style.

"There," he murmurs. Suddenly he puts a

gnarled hand on your shoulder and looks earnestly into your eyes. "Do you worship the one true God, little one?"

"Oh, yes," you answer softly. "There is no other!"

The man sighs, his barrel chest heaving. "Praise be to Him!" he cries. "Perhaps in His great mercy He will spare Nineveh. If only everyone in Nineveh repents, and calls upon God!"

Together you walk out into the dew-drenched early morning. Across golden wheat fields you see the ziggurat of Nineveh rising into the azure sky, the flowering shrubs on its terraces bright dots of color from this distance. Beside the ziggurat, the palace of the king soars imposingly. The old man turns suddenly to you.

"Run, youngster," he says urgently. "Go into the city, and make certain that everyone knows about repenting, and calling on God. No man or beast is to eat or drink and both man and beast must be covered in sackcloth!

"We shall meet again," he continues, a gentle smile softening the harsh lines of his weather-beaten face. "Whether now or later is in God's hands. Now hurry!"

You set off running toward the ziggurat, your lungs filling with the fresh, cool morning air. As you approach the rear of the palace courtyard, you notice that every man, woman, and child in view is wearing sackcloth. Donkeys plod slowly, their backs also covered in the coarse, black fabric. With a thrill of joy, you see the chariot of fire standing squarely in your path. Eagerly you scramble on board, bursting with questions.

A faint, faraway chime—like thousands of tiny bells—breaks the silence. "You have questions?" inquires the steed gently.

"Did *everyone* in Nineveh repent?" you ask breathlessly.

"Yes, little one," comes the soft answer.

"And did God destroy the city?" you ask more slowly.

"No, He did not," answers the steed. "God takes no pleasure in the death of the wicked, but rather that the wicked turn from evil and *live*. The people of Nineveh repented at the preaching of Jonah, and were spared.

"Now you must decide where you shall go next," continues the voice. "When the southern kingdom of Judah fell to Nebuchadnezzar, the prophet Ezekiel was captured and taken to Babylon with the second wave of captives—along with King Jehoiachin. I am allowed to take you to see Ezekiel on the forced march to Babylon, or to the town on the Chebar Canal outside of Babylon, where Ezekiel lived."

You wonder which choice might be more helpful on your quest, and take the reins thoughtfully in your hands. Pulling them taut, you choose your destination.

If you decide to see Ezekiel
taken to Babylon, go to page 83.

If you decide to go to the town in
Babylon where Ezekiel lived, go to page 87.

(You Have Come to See Sennacherib's Representative)

You are standing on a terraced wall that covers the side of a mountain ridge. As far as you can see, the wall bristles with well-armed soldiers. Wind whips your tunic, and a young soldier frowns at you.

"Where did you come from?" he growls. "No one should be up here without a weapon—here," he says, thrusting a wickedly sharp spear into your hands. "Sennacherib's army will not take our beloved Jerusalem without a fight!"

A heavily-armed Hebrew soldier hurries toward you both. "Come quickly!" he commands, his voice sharp with anger.

You jog after him, the spear feeling strange in your hand, until at last you enter a cool, stone tower built into the wall.

"Look down there!" the older soldier orders, pointing through a narrow gap in the stone toward the valley below.

Alone and unarmed at the foot of Jerusalem's wall stands a soldier—his tightly curled beard and pointed cap mark him as an Assyrian. He stands with his hands on his hips and his legs spread in an arrogant stance. Indeed, every line of his body suggests total arrogance. He cups his hands around his mouth and begins to shout; you are glad that the wind carries his words up to you.

"Hear the words of the great king of Assyria!" he roars. "Thus says the king, 'Do not let Hezekiah deceive you, for he will not be able to deliver you

from my hand! Do not let Hezekiah persuade you to trust in the Lord, saying, "The Lord will surely deliver us, and this city shall not be given into the hand of the king of Assyria."'"

The young soldier beside you gasps. "How dare he speak like that about King Hezekiah?"

"How dare he speak like that about the Lord?" mutters the other, his mouth a grim straight line.

You all strain to listen as Sennacherib's representative continues. "Do not let Hezekiah mislead you when he says, 'The Lord will deliver us.' Has the god of any nation ever delivered his land from the hand of the king of Assyria? Who of all the gods of these countries has been able to save his land from Assyria? How then can the Lord deliver Jerusalem?"

The wind moans eerily around the stone tower, but you hear no one answer the arrogant Assyrian. "Why doesn't someone answer him?" you question angrily.

"Because King Hezekiah has commanded us not to," explains the older soldier. "Come, youngster. I have a feeling that the prophet Isaiah will have an answer for the mighty king of Assyria. My duties are finished for the day and I have a mind to visit Isaiah. Will you accompany me?"

Nodding eagerly, you join the old soldier as he descends from the wall into the city of Jerusalem and begins winding through a maze of narrow streets.

"Ah!" your companion breathes. "Look! King Hezekiah's most trusted servants are just now entering the house of the prophet!"

You look at the three men hurrying into the doorway of a house across the street. Rough sackcloth covers their tunics, and their faces are tight with worry.

"Come," says your companion with a kind smile. "There is always a welcome in Isaiah's home for those who love the Lord!"

Together you step into the entry and follow a dim hall until it opens into a spacious courtyard. Water gurgles in a large stone fountain in the center, and a tall man listens intently to the king's servants. You are surprised at Isaiah's appearance, for he is not in

mourning and his clothing is that of a nobleman.
You realize that you had expected the prophet to be
poor, and then you remember that Isaiah may have
actually been related to King Hezekiah himself. You
and your companion cross the courtyard to stand
quietly behind the three men in sackcloth.

"Tell your master," says Isaiah calmly, "this is
what the Lord says, 'Do not be afraid of what you
have heard—those words with which the servants
of the king of Assyria have blasphemed me. Listen!
I will put a spirit in him so that when he hears a
rumor, he will return to his own country, and there
I will cut him down with the sword.'"

Excitement surges through you as you realize that you have heard with your own ears *two* prophecies: Sennacherib will hear a rumor and return to this own land, *and* he will fall by the sword in his own land.

Isaiah and the other men are speaking quietly when you notice the chariot standing silently at the edge of the courtyard. Quickly you race toward it and scramble in behind the steed. You look once more at the face of the prophet Isaiah before the flames engulf you.

"Will Sennacherib attack Jerusalem this time?" you ask eagerly.

"No, my friend, for the Lord's word is true," answers the voice. "Isaiah knows that Jerusalem is in no danger and that is why he is not wearing sackcloth. But Sennacherib's army will come against the city again, and then the Lord will send His angel to stop it. Here is your choice: You may go to the time of Sennacherib's death, or you may witness his second attempt to march against Jerusalem."

You realize with a thrill that you are going to be able to see prophecy fulfilled either way you decide. You take the reins in hand, and make your decision.

If you decide to see
the death of Sennacherib, go to page 51.

If you decide to see Sennacherib's
second attack, go to page 43.

(You Have Decided to Go to Isaiah and Hezekiah)

You are standing in a pool of shadows in a large, columned room. Heavy wooden shutters have been drawn across the windows, and the jewels inlaid in tall wooden chests that line one wall wink dully in the dim light. A low moan makes you shiver, and you turn to see a man tossing uneasily on an ornate bed. Crumpled blankets spill off the bed onto the floor. *A king suffers like any other man when he is sick,* you think.

The door opens suddenly, and you recognize Isaiah. He calmly crosses the thick rug laid over the cold stone floor, and stops beside the bed. Isaiah places his hand gently on the king's forehead, and you see anguish and pain on Hezekiah's face as he looks steadily at the prophet.

"This is what the Lord says," Isaiah reports softly, "'Put your house in order, because you are going to die; you will not recover.'"

Hezekiah's eyes widen with fear and he turns his face toward the wall. Isaiah looks at him steadily for a moment, then turns abruptly to leave. The prophet's direct gaze meets yours, and he beckons. You follow him uncomfortably out the door, reaching to close it behind you. Faintly, the king's voice reaches you.

"Remember, O Lord, how I have walked before you faithfully and with wholehearted devotion, and have done what is good in your eyes," quavers Hezekiah. You close the door softly and follow the retreating form of the prophet.

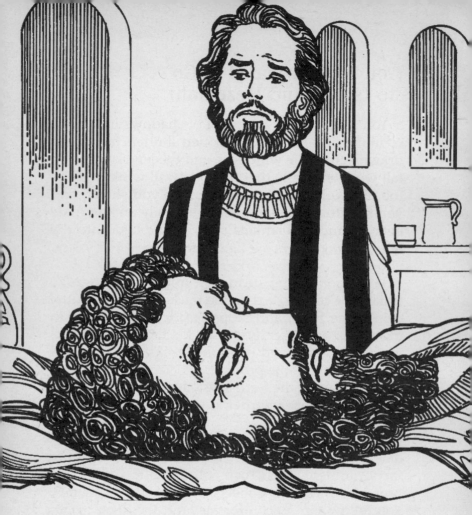

Beautifully carved wooden panels, polished to a high sheen and inlaid with ivory and jewels, glow softly in the muted light, and direct you through a wide doorway into an oasis of flowering shrubs and shade trees. A huge stone fountain gurgles musically, and servants hurry across the courtyard. All eyes are on Isaiah as he calmly strides through the lush garden and out through the door in the opposite wall. You stand uncertainly, wondering what you should do now.

"The king is dying, isn't he?" a wide-eyed servant girl whispers. "What does the prophet say?" she questions as she looks anxiously at you. Before you can reply, Isaiah returns to the courtyard. An ancient servant, his back twisted and bowed, tugs respectfully on the prophet's sleeve. Isaiah smiles kindly at him.

"Prepare a poultice of figs and apply it to the king's boil, and he will recover," he says softly to the old man.

The servant's face lights up with relief, and he hurries off. "Take a fig poultice to the king instantly!" his thin old voice floats across the courtyard.

You fall into step behind Isaiah as he retraces his steps toward the king's bedchamber. The polished panels of the hall disappear in the leaping flames of the chariot.

"Here is your choice," says the steed quietly. "You may see what happens to Hezekiah, or you may go more than one hundred years into the future to see the fall of Jerusalem predicted by Isaiah."

Keeping your quest in mind, you make your decision.

If you decide to see what happens to Hezekiah, go to page 40.

If you decide to see the fall of Jerusalem, go to page 104.

(You Have Decided to See
What Happens to King Hezekiah)

You are back in the bedchamber of King Hezekiah. The king is sitting bolt upright in bed, one trembling hand outstretched to Isaiah. The faithful old servant hovers near the king's bedside, hope and despair struggling in his face.

Isaiah smiles as he delivers his message, "This is what the Lord, the God of your father David, says: 'I have heard your prayer and seen your tears; I will add fifteen years to your life. And I will deliver you and this city from the hand of the king of Assyria.'"

"But . . ." the king stammers, "what will be the sign that the Lord will heal me?"

A hush falls over everyone present as all eyes turn to Isaiah. "This is the Lord's sign to you that the Lord will do what He has promised: the shadow cast by the sun will go back the ten steps it has gone down on the stairway of Ahaz," Isaiah answers softly as he motions toward a window beside Hezekiah's bed.

The king smiles slightly as the servant hurries over to throw the heavy wooden shutters wide open. Sunshine streams into the room, and everyone draws close to the king's bed. You stand on your toes to look out the window at the courtyard below.

Broad stone stairs lead from the palace to the huge paved garden; servants hurry beneath the columned portico that lines the courtyard on three sides. The sun slants down from behind the palace, casting a shadow which reaches halfway down the wide steps.

Hezekiah turns to Isaiah. "It is easy for the shadow to decline ten steps, but to see it turn backward ten steps . . ." he says in an awed whisper, "no, this has never been seen."

You jump in startled surprise as Isaiah utters a cry, his head tilted back and his face turned heavenward. As you peer intently out the window, your knees suddenly feel like water. Impossibly, incredibly, the shadow on the steps below has changed direction. The black shadow creeps up one step, then two, then three. A sharp intake of breath and you hear someone murmur "four." Awed silence throbs like a presence as you all watch the shadow move—against all physical possibilities—*backward* up nine steps. Ashen faces flicker in the shaded portico below, and you find you are holding your breath. "Ten," murmurs Hezekiah and the shadow ceases movement.

Flames engulf you, and you see the courtyard no more. You exhale shakily, your knees still weak. You will not soon forget what you have seen this day!

You are so awed that you almost fail to hear the soft bell-like voice of the steed. "Your choice now is between the present and more than one hundred years in the future. You may meet the prophet Micah, who prophesied at the same time as Isaiah, or you may go forward in time to the fall of Jerusalem, predicted by Isaiah."

You know that you have already accomplished part of your quest—you have seen with your own eyes that the prophecies came true! You still must discover if all prophets were chosen by God; perhaps the prophet Micah might answer that, you reflect. Thoughtfully, you make your decision and pull the reins taut.

If you decide to meet the prophet Micah, go to page 62.

If you decide to see the fall of Jerusalem, go to page 104.

(You Have Decided to See Sennacherib's Second Attack)

You find yourself outside in a pitch-black night. No moon is visible overhead, and a silence filled with dread seems to lie like a blanket over the area. As you strain to see in the darkness, you recognize the stepped walls and turrets of the city of Jerusalem. You step back, and a startled cry makes your heart skip a beat.

"Halt!" quavers a man's voice. A white face looms close to yours in the inky dark, and you recognize the younger soldier you met when you saw Sennacherib's representative.

"Oh, it's you," he sighs. "I thank Almighty God that it will soon be dawn—this has been a night I will never forget!"

"Why?" you whisper nervously, wondering uneasily why this night feels so ominous.

You can feel the young soldier shudder. "Look down there," he breathes, pointing to the valley below. "The troops of the king of Assyria pitched their camp there for the final assault on Jerusalem, but their campfires died out hours ago—why? No army would allow their fires to die out! And this silence! Something very strange is about to happen. I can feel it in the very air I breathe!"

The lonely, sobbing howl of a jackal punctuates the stillness, and your heart begins to hammer as other wild cries join in an eerie, distant chorus.

The soldier beside you gasps. "I have never heard so many jackals at once," he whispers. "There must be many dead somewhere!"

The sky begins to lighten ever so slightly near the eastern horizon. You stare anxiously at the blurred scene below, noting that there are thousands upon thousands of tents, stretching out as far as you look. An agonized wail echoes suddenly in the valley and other terrified wail sends chills up your spine. You shudder as more screams of horror burst from throats below. The face of the soldier beside you is

chalky-white, but his eyes are wide with wonder. "Isaiah's prophecy!" he says. "Isaiah said that Sennacherib would not come into this city, that the Lord himself would defend Jerusalem. Look!"

You follow the direction of his pointing finger, and freeze in awe. There in the valley below, thousands of Assyrian soldiers lie motionless on the ground. A handful of their terrified companions

wander dazedly around the lifeless forms; others stagger crazily from tents, howls of stark terror erupting madly. A series of shaky trumpet blasts sound, and you see a group of men spring onto the backs of their waiting horses.

"That is Sennacherib himself," exclaims your companion.

"How do you know that?" you breathe.

Your companion grins at you triumphantly. "That is the king's banner," he answers, pointing to a purple and gold flag fluttering from a staff being carried by the group of men. Their horses proceed slowly, picking their way carefully through the sea of bodies.

"Praise be to the Lord most high!" shouts a voice behind you.

Hundreds of rejoicing Hebrew soldiers take up the cry, until it seems that the mountains must split with the sound of praise. The sun bursts into sight in the eastern sky, sending golden fingers of radiance across the walls of the city of Jerusalem, saved by God himself.

The breathtaking scene shimmers for an instant, then disappears as you find yourself once more in the chariot.

"You will be allowed to see the prophet Isaiah again," says the voice of the steed. "You may go forward in time to learn of Isaiah's prediction *by name* of the Persian king who will issue the decree allowing the Hebrews to return to their land from captivity in Babylon."

"Wait, though," you stammer haltingly. "That wasn't too hard to do, was it? I mean, wouldn't

Isaiah have known who was king of Persia?"

Bell-like chimes fill the air. "No, little one, not then. The destruction of Jerusalem lasted twenty years and took place eighty to one hundred years after Isaiah's death. The first captives taken to Babylon included the king, Jehoiachin, the prophet Ezekiel—and some young men named Daniel, Hananiah, Mishael, and Azariah. When Jerusalem was completely destroyed, more captives were held in Babylon until it was destroyed by the Medes and the Persians fifty years after that. Without God's help, how could any human have known who would be the king of Persia more than one hundred and fifty years into the future?"

Your head swims as you digest this information. "So some of the Israelites were captives in Babylon for seventy years, right? And Daniel became a prophet while he was in Babylon, right?"

"You are learning well, little one. Remember those names and figures. But right now, your alternative destination is to go back in time right here in Jerusalem, to hear several prophecies that Isaiah has for King Hezekiah—one of which you have already seen fulfilled! Which destination shall you choose?"

Marveling over the wonder of fulfilled prophecy, you take the reins in hand and decide.

If you decide to hear Isaiah's prediction about the Persian king, go to page 55.

If you decide to hear Isaiah's predictions concerning Hezekiah, go to page 37.

(You Have Come to Nahum's Village)

You duck as a small, greenish-yellow, pear-shaped fruit bounces off your head—you are standing beneath a quivering tree and fruits are raining down on you. Hurrying out from underneath the tree, you see a man shaking it vigorously. He stops and picks up a leather bag, stooping to pick up the fruits that have been shaken loose.

You gather up several and place them in his bag, and he looks up at you with a grateful smile. You ask, "Could you please tell me how to find Nahum the prophet?"

Penetrating dark eyes bore into your own as he replies, "You have found him, youngster."

Suddenly tongue-tied, you realize that you aren't certain what you should ask him! You remember that Nahum predicted that Nineveh would be destroyed, so you summon up your courage and ask, "Do you have a prophecy against Nineveh?"

His dark eyes flash, and he flings the leather sack down upon the ground. "Woe to that bloody city, full of lies!" he thunders. "Oh, yes—I have a prophecy!"

"Is Nineveh so very wicked?" you ask timidly. Nahum's flashing dark eyes soften, and he draws you to sit beside him on a flat rock beneath the shade of the tree. "Listen, youngster—and I will tell you about the cruelty of Nineveh, though it is not a tale for weak stomachs!" His gaze faraway, Nahum's mouth twists with disgust. "Pyramids of human heads warn those who resist the Assyrian army—men are skinned alive. Other victims are impaled on long poles, which are then driven into the ground and the victim left to die. Women and children are carried into slavery, and the city unlucky enough to be captured by the Assyrian army is plundered and burned. Thus does the mighty Nineveh do to her conquests!"

Your stomach churns as Nahum asks quietly, "Do you want me to go on? There is more . . . ."

You shake your head, sickened by what you have heard.

"But the Lord God gave me a vision," says Nahum. "Like those who are drunken, Nineveh will be destroyed. With an overflowing flood He will make a complete end of its site. The gates of her land will be opened wide to her enemies, and she will be total desolation and waste!"

You listen carefully, trying to commit all that Nahum has told you to memory. The prophet glances at the twisted trunk of the fruit tree. "Did you see how easily the figs fell as I shook the tree?" he asks, his piercing eyes fastened intently on your face.

"Yes," you reply, wondering at his sudden change of subject.

"All of Nineveh's fortifications are fig trees with ripe fruit—when shaken, they fall into the eater's mouth," continues the prophet. He rises, gathering the leather sack and flinging it over his shoulder in one fluid motion. "Remember, my friend," says Nahum, "All that the Lord speaks will happen— just as He says it will!"

Nahum strides toward a dusty road, and waves

farewell. You wave in return and are not surprised to see the milky white steed standing quietly beneath the fig tree, its flaming chariot glowing. Thoughtfully, you climb inside.

"I think," you begin slowly, "that there were four parts to that prophecy."

The familiar bell-like voice replies, "You are correct, little one."

Counting off thoughtfully on your fingers, you continue, "Nineveh will be destroyed like those who are drunken, and the city will be destroyed in an overflowing flood — that's two specific prophecies. She will be burned, and she will be totally destroyed — that's four, right?"

"Right again," the steed answers approvingly. "Mark well what you have learned, for here is your choice. You may go to the site of an archaeological dig in 1858, or you may go to see the fall of Nineveh in 607 B.C."

You have an uncomfortable feeling that the fall of Nineveh will not be an especially pleasant sight, but you wonder how visiting an archaeological dig will help you on your quest. You pull the reins taut and make your decision.

If you decide to go to the
archaeological dig, go to page 131.

If you decide to see the fall
of Nineveh, go to page 73.

(You Have Decided to See the Death of Sennacherib)

Deep shadows lie in pools on a cold marble floor. You are standing behind a huge, carved pillar. Peering cautiously out, you see a forest of similar columns in a vast room. At the front, a huge golden statue gleams dully in an enclosure flanked by the guttering flames of torches. A deadly silence throbs, and the hair on the back of your neck prickles uncomfortably.

You edge carefully around the pillars, your feet making no noise on the polished marble — until at last you are close to the front of the room. From here you can see a bloody altar directly in front of the statue and a man lying prostrate before it. The golden image of the pagan goddess is revolting. The whispered prayers of the man on the floor echo eerily in the cold, stone room. His clothing is richly decorated, and an ornate crown (looking like a fez topped with a cone) nestles on his jet-black curls. *This must be King Sennacherib*, you think.

You suddenly become aware of a subtle change in the shadows; uneasily, you press yourself against the pillar. Hoping fervently that you are concealed in the dim corner, you search the shadows in the room carefully. As your eyes become more accustomed to the strange light, you see two men creeping stealthily from column to column. Your heart hammering, you watch in silence as they advance closer to the prostrate king. Their drawn swords glitter in the torchlight, and pure hatred sparks in their dark eyes.

Sennacherib scrambles suddenly to his feet, whirling around and crouching tensely. Shock and horror struggle on his face as he sees the two men. "You!" he shrieks, as the attackers lunge forward.

You press your hands tightly against your mouth. The swords drive home, and the king of Assyria falls to his knees, his hands clutching his chest. Blood gushes from the wounds between his hands, quickly soaking his garments.

"My sons," he whispers. "My sons . . . . " The

death rattle sounds in his throat, and Sennacherib shudders and crumples to the ground.

"Well, Adrammelech," sneers one of the men "The deed is done. Now all we have to do is remove our dear brother Esarhaddon from the land of the living, and the throne of Assyria will belong to us!"

The other's narrowed eyes flick over the fallen king carelessly. "Let's be certain this job is finished first, Sharezer," he replies. He kicks the lifeless form of his father roughly, then plunges his sword once again into the still body.

Adrammelech's cruel laugh rings out, echoing horribly. "By all means, brother! Let us have no more trouble with this king." His sword, too, slices into the fallen Sennacherib, then the two of them wipe their bloodied swords on the robes of the dead king.

They straighten quickly, sheathing their weapons. With a cautious glance over their shoulders, they melt swiftly into the shadows and disappear.

You almost shout with relief as the dancing flames surround you, mercifully blotting the dead king from your sight. Sick as you are, you realize suddenly that you have once again seen a prophecy literally fulfilled, for Isaiah said that Sennacherib would die by the sword in his own land!

"I am allowed to take you to learn about yet another of Isaiah's prophecies," says the steed softly. "You may decide to join a merchant of this time traveling to the city of Petra—or you may see Petra in the twentieth century. Which shall you choose?"

Petra? you puzzle. You have no idea which choice would help you more on your quest, so you make your decision carelessly.

If you decide to join the merchant on his way to Petra, go to page 100.

If you decide to see Petra in the twentieth century, go to page 139.

(You Have Decided to Hear Isaiah's Prediction)

You find yourself back in the pleasant courtyard of Isaiah. Men and women crowd around the prophet, their faces reflecting mingled triumph and bewilderment.

"But how can that be?" pleads a young woman. "The Lord himself halted the king of Assyria and his army at the very gates of Jerusalem. Now you are telling us that our city will be captured by the Babylonians?"

An older man interrupts, his heavy grey brows almost meeting over his nose in a frown. "How can you say that the Babylonians will be able to defeat us, when the Assyrians could not? This makes no sense at all, Isaiah!"

Isaiah surveys the crowd patiently. "Did you say that the Assyrians could not defeat *us*, Nathan?" he asks gently.

The older man flushes. "Alright, alright!" he mutters gruffly. "They would have taken Jerusalem unless the Lord himself had stopped them. But you know what I mean, prophet," he continues. "Babylon is only a vassal state of Assyria—how can we be in danger from them?"

Isaiah smiles at the confused people facing him. "I tell you the word of the Lord, my friends. The Lord has declared what He will do before it happens—that way all the world may know that He is God. Can an idol of stone or wood tell you what is going to happen? Of course not! But the Lord has told you that Jerusalem will fall to Babylon and that

Babylon will be destroyed by the Medes and the Persians. After the people of Israel are held captive in Babylon, Cyrus, the king of Persia, shall declare that Jerusalem will be rebuilt!"

"Who is Cyrus?" murmurs a woman, her brow puckered in a frown. "Jerusalem's walls are unbroken today. Are you saying that our beautiful city will be completely destroyed?"

Through the babble of voices you hear the quiet, musical tones of your steed. "You have heard the prophecy—now here is your choice. You may see the fulfillment of the prophecy, when Cyrus the Great issues his decree; or you may see the fall of Babylon. Which will be your choice?"

You remember that Babylon fell to Cyrus in 536 B.C., more than one hundred years after Isaiah's prophecy! Wondering which decision might help you more, you think carefully, and choose.

If you decide to hear Cyrus issue the decree, go to page 111.

If you decide to see the fall of Babylon, go to page 107.

(You Have Decided to Go
   Forward in Time to Babylon)

You find yourself straining to see in the dim shadows of a small room. Perspiration stands in beads on your forehead because the fire in the large hearth has heated the room to an uncomfortably warm temperature. Wiping the sweat from your forehead with your forearm, you look curiously around the room. A thick-set man bends attentively over the fire, blowing the glowing coals carefully through a long clay pipe. He turns suddenly, and scowls ferociously.

"Where have you been?" he roars, his brows meeting over his nose in a fierce frown. "I have paid for your services for the *full* day, and you're late! Here—take over the blowpipe!" His complaints continue in a sullen murmur as he thrusts the long pipe into your hands.

You bend over the terrible heat, blowing obediently through the pipe. The coals spark, and the man whirls in irritation. "Not like that, idiot!" he snarls. "Gently! Do you want to catch on fire?"

Watching the embers warily through stinging eyes, you blow more carefully. The man hurries over, moving a long-handled ladle containing a chunk of what looks like gold into the hottest part of the fire.

"There," he mutters, fitting the handle of the ladle into a notch cut into the side of the hearth. He bustles away again, this time returning with a clay pot filled with sand into which molds have been set. He places the pot over the white-hot coals, and moves away with a satisfied sigh.

"Keep blowing!" he says sharply, but the irritation has faded from his face. "These little statues must be ready for the priest by sundown—but I think we'll make it."

You are so hot and thirsty by now that you almost don't notice that your face feels like it is on fire. At last, the man carefully lifts the ladle of molten gold and pours its contents into the little forms set in the sand. He motions you to stop blowing, and you step gratefully away from the fire.

"I am Kudda," he says with a grin. "And you didn't do too badly, my friend."

You slump gratefully beside him on a stone bench, and gulp thirstily the cup of water Kudda hands you.

"My son usually helps me," he says slowly, "but he was just too sick to work today. And the priests do not wait!"

A knock resounds on the wooden door, and Kudda springs to his feet and crosses the room.

"The priests," Kudda growls in annoyance as he flings open the door.

Two men, their shaven heads gleaming with scented oil, glide into the room. Their eyes are narrow with suspicion as they glance swiftly around the small workroom. "Not finished yet, Kudda?" one inquires smoothly.

You suddenly realize that so far, all you have seen of Babylon has been the inside of this tiny room and it occurs to you that this might be a good opportunity for you to escape. Quietly you edge out the open door into the street beyond—and stand frozen to the spot in amazement!

The clean lines of three- and four-story buildings soar skyward, clustered together like the downtown of a twentieth-century city. A broad street paved with massive stones runs straight between the rows of buildings, and throngs of people bustle past. The buildings' saw-tooth walls look almost striped, as the dark, vertical shadows alternate with smooth, whitewashed stone. A rhythmic boom echoes off the buildings, and you move down the street in the direction of the sound.

A crowd of people streams into a dark doorway and you follow—entering a dim hallway. Rounding a corner, you move past dark passages branching off in two directions; you follow the group into a large courtyard. The rhythmic booming sounds painfully loud now, and you see that it is coming from a huge kettle drum in the center of the courtyard. Startled, you also see several men leaping in the air around the drum, their leopard-skin coverings whirling as they dance. The heads of the leopards bob crazily on each shaven head, being anchored beneath their chins with leather thongs.

"Why are they doing that?" you whisper to a Babylonian man standing nearby.

He turns a wide, astonished gaze upon you. "Did you not know that tonight we are to have a total eclipse of the moon?"

You shake your head, and he continues. "They must drive away the demons that cause the eclipse, of course. I fear this night!" he hisses, shuddering.

The insistent drum beat is beginning to make your head throb, and you slip away toward the street. A clean white glow lights up one dark passage, and your heart leaps to see the chariot of fire waiting for you. Eagerly, you scramble into the chariot.

"It is time for you to make a decision," says the steed softly. "I am allowed to take you to see Ezekiel on the forced march to Babylon, or to the town on the Chebar Canal outside of Babylon, where Ezekiel lived."

Thoughtfully, you pick up the reins. Pulling them taut, you make your decision.

If you decide to see Ezekiel being taken to Babylon, go to page 83.

If you decide to go to the town in Babylon where Ezekiel lived, go to page 87.

(You Have Decided
to Meet the Prophet Micah)

A tug on your tunic almost makes you lose your balance. You look down to see that you are standing in the middle of a flock of goats and one is contentedly chewing the fabric of your tunic. Gently, you remove the soggy cloth from the goat's mouth as it bleats in protest. Ahead, several children surround a man sitting in the shade of a tree, and you make your way toward him.

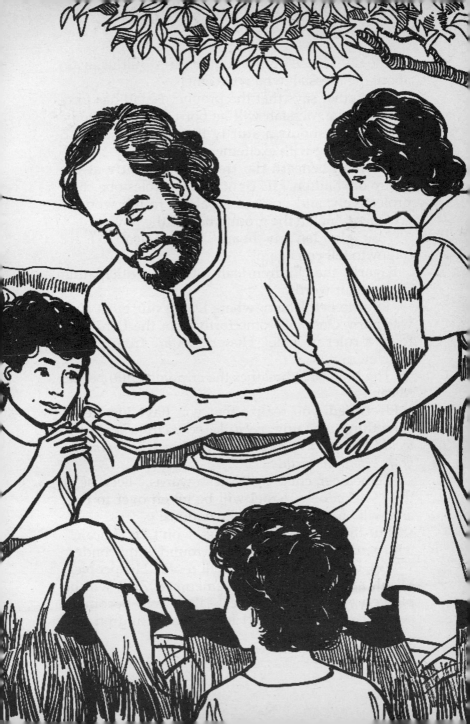

"Please, Micah!" pipes a little girl. "Tell us again about the Messiah who will come!"

"My father says that the prophet Isaiah has foretold that the Messiah will be born of King David's royal line!" shouts a sturdy little boy, his brown eyes sparkling with excitement.

The man beneath the tree smiles gently at the group of children. His right arm encircles one child protectively, and you see a pair of rough wooden crutches lying on the ground beside the boy.

"You gladden my heart," says Micah. "I am happy to tell you again!"

Eagerly, the children lean forward, anticipating the familiar words.

"In little Bethlehem, where David our great king was born, One will come forth from the Lord God to be a ruler in Israel. His origins are from of old, from eternity!"

"The Messiah!" breathes the crippled child beside Micah.

Electrified, you realize that you have just heard something amazing; *even the very city where Jesus would be born was foretold more than seven hundred years before His birth!*

"Remember, children!" Micah warns, "Because of their wickedness, Israel will be given over to ruin and will bear the scorn of the nations!"

"But the Lord will rescue us, won't He, Micah?" whispers the little girl, her eyes round with wonder.

"Yes, child, of course He will rescue His people," Micah replies softly. "But remember, Zion will be plowed as a field, and Jerusalem will become a heap of ruins. You must teach your children and your children's children to beware of false prophets who lead the Lord's people astray. The diviners and the seers will be ashamed because there is no answer from God!"

The little girl creeps close to the prophet, putting her chubby arm around his neck lovingly. "We'll remember, dear Micah," she says softly.

The sight disappears as you find yourself back in the chariot. Amazed at what you have just heard, you pick up the reins absently.

"Your journey is almost finished," says the steed. "I take you now to the temple of the Lord in Jerusalem, at the very time of Christ's betrayal."

Go to page 122.

(You Have Decided to Go Backward to Ezekiel's Prophecy)

You find yourself in a small courtyard. Moonlight drenches the whitewashed walls, and the leaves of a tiny fruit tree rustle soothingly. You recognize the solitary figure of Ezekiel, the prophet, slumped wearily on a low stone bench. His magnificent mane of hair and thick beard have been shaved, but still the dark brows jut over his piercing eyes. He lifts his head suddenly, and looks directly at you.

"Yes, my child?" he asks gently.

Swallowing nervously, you slowly approach the mighty prophet. Pain has carved deep lines on his face and you see wells of sorrow in his eyes. "I don't mean to intrude," you begin—

"Do you love the Lord God?" Ezekiel interrupts, his flashing eyes searching your face intently.

You nod speechlessly, overcome by the sheer force of a prophet used so mightily by God.

Ezekiel's face softens. "His light shines in your face, child. Come, sit here with me," he says softly.

You sit in silence for a few moments, listening in pleasure to the sleepy sounds of birds settling in for the night and the rustle of leaves in the gentle night breeze. At length, Ezekiel sighs.

"What happened to your hair?" you whisper, darting an uneasy sidelong glance at the prophet's unevenly-shorn head.

"The Lord God told me to take a sword and use it as a barber's razor on my head and beard," he answers simply.

"But *why*?" you protest.

"As an illustration of what is going to happen to Jerusalem," Ezekiel answers quietly. "One third of my hair I burned, one third I struck with the sword, and one third I scattered to the wind."

The prophet glances at your puzzled face and continues. "That means that one third of Jerusalem's citizens will die by fire in the coming siege, one third will die by the sword, and the remaining third will be scattered to the wind."

"Will Jerusalem fall?" you whisper.

The prophet's eyes look far away. "Oh yes, Jerusalem will fall," he replies slowly. "The Lord has set me to be a watchman on the wall."

You stiffen to attention. "What does that mean?"

Ezekiel smiles. "A city must have watchmen on her walls, to spot any enemy who might invade while her people sleep," he replies. "The prophets sound the alarm of God's judgements to come to the sleeping children of Israel so that they may awake to repentance and obedience."

"But why?" you whisper sadly. "Why must Jerusalem be destroyed?"

Ezekiel's eyes flash. "The house of Judah has committed abominations in the temple; Judah and

Israel have filled the land with violence. They rebel against the Lord continually, and worship pagan idols of stone and wood!"

You shiver at his words, and ask hesitantly, "Are all prophets appointed by God?"

Ezekiel springs to his feet and the moon above casts the shadow of his broad shoulders on the stone courtyard. "All *true* prophets are appointed by God, child. But not everyone who calls himself or herself a prophet is appointed by the Lord God."

You gasp involuntarily at the magnitude of this sin. "You mean there are people who say they are prophets, but they're *not*?"

Ezekiel paces like a caged lion in the moonlit garden. "Woe to those foolish prophets! They see visions of peace for Jerusalem when there is no peace!" he roars. "They are following their own spirit and have seen nothing! They see falsehood and lying divination, and say 'The Lord declares,' when the Lord has *not* sent them! They hope for the fulfillment of *their* word!"

"How do they *dare*?" you murmur, aghast.

Suddenly radiance floods the quiet garden as the chariot of fire appears silently. Ezekiel smiles gently. "You must go now, little one. We shall meet again one day—cling to the word of the Lord!"

You take one last look at the mighty prophet of God before climbing into the chariot. Dancing flames surround you and the voice chimes, "I take you now to witness the fall of Jerusalem."

Shivering, you take up the reins and wait.

Go to page 104.

(You Have Decided to Go to Nineveh in 630 B.C.)

Soft music floats gently in the cool dusk and you look around with interest. Neat rows of date palms are banked with flowering shrubs, and the bracing scent of pine makes the air smell clean. In the center of these well-ordered grounds you see servants bustling around some grape vines that form a canopy over several figures. You edge nearer, hoping to get a better look at the man reclining beneath the canopy.

"Here—take this!" hisses a voice behind you, and a long pole with brilliant peacock feathers at the end is thrust into your hands. "Hurry! Surely you know how Assurbanipal hates flies!"

The harassed servant hurries away, and you approach the royal party in the center of the park. You steal a look at the king, and shudder at the cruelty etched in deep lines on his face; the queen's mouth droops in a pout, as she waves away a fly.

"You!" she whines, pointing an accusing finger straight at you. "If you do not wish to lose your head, you had best keep these troublesome flies away from me!"

Your heart hammering, you hurry to stand behind her carved throne, waving the royal fly-whisk briskly behind her. The king watches his wife with amusement, his mouth twisting into a sneer.

"Why are you so irritable, my dear?" purrs the king softly. "Do you not enjoy my decorations for our evening meal?"

Decorations? you puzzle, looking out of the corner of your eye around the peaceful garden.

The queen smiles, her spoiled mouth twisting unpleasantly. "Of course, my king," she answers. "But I enjoyed the head of the king of Elam more!"

A servant bearing a silver platter piled high with fruit jerks nervously, and you see the blood drain from his frightened face. His eyes dart in terror to the face of the king.

"This talk of heads is making our servant nervous, wife," says the king with a careless laugh.

The queen frowns at the trembling servant. "Away with you," she snaps. "That chalky face of yours will spoil my dinner! Perhaps it would look better on a pole!"

The man's face freezes in petrified horror and he backs hastily away, bobbing up and down in jerky bows. The queen's cruel laugh rings hollowly. *What is all this talk about heads?* you wonder, as you continue looking around you carefully.

Suddenly your heart leaps into your throat—for there, several feet away and almost hidden behind a palm tree, is a human head impaled on a pole. Blood roars in your ears, and you struggle against the waves of horror washing over you. The glassy stare of cold, dead eyes freezes you to your very marrow—*how could any human being take pleasure in such evil*? The fly-whisk falls from your slack hands, and you turn on your heel and stumble away from the canopy. Shouts fade into the distance as you are surrounded by the pure flames of the chariot. Sick and revolted, you lean against the side.

"The Assyrian empire was one of the most wicked in history," says the voice of the steed, "And also one of the most powerful. The walls of Nineveh were one hundred feet high, her soldiers were veterans, and she had the full might of a highly trained and well-organized military machine. You have seen for yourself the cruelty of this empire," the voice continues. "Now I am permitted to take you to the village of Nahum the prophet. Mark well what you learn there!"

Still shaken by what you have seen, you pick up the reins and wait.

Go to page 48.

(You Have Come to See the Fall of Nineveh)

Triumphant shouts pound your ears and you look down from a high battlement onto a swirling sea of jubilant soldiers below. The gates set into the hundred-foot-high walls of Nineveh have crumbled, and cavalry swarms across the nearby river to ride unchecked into the city. A sea of riders in scarlet caps splashes vibrant color on the plain below as they thunder into the city, spears at the ready. Glittering chariots rumble side-by-side behind the cavalry and you hear the shrieks of terrified citizens who are just discovering that their proud, cruel city is falling.

A vise-like grip on your arm makes you jump, and you look into the grim face of a middle-aged woman. "Come, youngster," she says firmly, "this is no place for either of us now." She propels you forward, and you decide not to resist. You may learn something from her that would help you on your quest. Without speaking, you hurry together down broad stone steps and into a dark, narrow passageway.

"The Medes and Persians aren't likely to find this passageway for a while," she whispers. "We may yet escape this city before it is too late!"

"I thought that Nineveh was practically impossible to conquer," you pant as you jog after her.

The woman snorts. "It has *never* been overrun!" she snaps. "And now—after a siege of only three months—the city will be taken!"

"Three months is a long siege, isn't it?" you ask.

The woman stops to stare at you, her mouth agape.

"Long! It is unheard of — a wink of time! Why, many sieges take more than twenty *years*. But the king should have known this would happen," she mutters darkly.

The passageway has grown so narrow that you are forced to follow behind the woman, and you realize that you are still descending. You see her shoulders brush the walls in the increasing gloom, and a damp and musty smell tickles your nostrils.

"Where are we?" you whisper uncomfortably.

The woman turns, a finger on her lips warningly. "Under the river," she breathes. "Hush now. We must not be caught!"

Total darkness seems to press down on you like a weight and breathing becomes more difficult in the stale air of the tunnel. You recoil in disgust as your hands brush accidentally against the walls, slippery with mildew. After what seems like hours, the passage widens once more — and begins to climb. Daylight glows at the end of the corridor, and you step forward to walk beside the hurrying woman.

"Why should the king have known that Nineveh would be overrun?" you question curiously.

Your companion smiles grimly. "Two reasons, really," she answers slowly. "Three months ago, the king was camped outside the city with his army, ready to defend Nineveh. But he was so sure that no one would ever be able to take his city that he grew careless." She laughs without mirth, and continues, "The king and his soldiers began to enjoy themselves in feasting, and much wine. In short, they were so drunk that when the enemy attacked, they had to flee inside the gates of Nineveh—and many brave Assyrian soldiers were lost!"

You listen in horrified fascination, realizing that *this was in exact fulfillment of Nahum's prophecy that like those who are drunken they are consumed*! Eagerly you ask, "What was the second reason that the king should have known that Nineveh would be destroyed?"

The woman pauses at the daylight-flooded opening of the corridor. Her gaze is faraway as she replies, "Our people have had a prophecy for many years that no enemy will ever take Nineveh by storm unless the river shall first become the city's enemy. Come, and look!" she says, tugging urgently at your arm and pulling you out into the daylight.

Blinking in the sunshine after the dimness of the tunnel, you see that you are standing on a low rise of ground. Across the river you see the imposing walls of Nineveh, punctuated by towers twice the height of the walls. You look at the crumbled city gates and notice that the river has washed away the supports for a long segment of the mighty walls. Water surges through a swollen bed, eroding the foundation of the protecting city walls.

"Do you see?" the woman says, her voice rising shrilly. "Heavy rains have swelled the river—the river itself has become the enemy, and has broken down part of her walls!"

Gooseflesh prickles on your arms as you realize you are seeing for yourself another part of Nahum's fulfilled prophecy: *With an overflowing*

flood, God will make a complete end of Nineveh's site! You look in awe at the sight across the river; black smoke curls into the air, and sun gleams off flashing swords.

"I must flee!" the woman hisses urgently, as she turns and scurries off, looking furtively back over her shoulder.

The pure flames of the chariot surround you, and you see Nineveh no more. You sink gratefully back, and listen for the voice of your steed.

"You have no decision to make this time," says the voice. "I shall take you back in time, to see the Assyrian King Sennacherib's representative at the gates of Jerusalem."

"Will I hear another prophecy?" you ask eagerly.

The steed's chiming laughter tinkles softly. "Yes, little one, you shall."

Anxious to learn more, you take the reins hurriedly in your hands and pull them taut.

Go to page 31.

(You Have Decided to Go to Ezekiel's Home)

A crush of bodies surrounds you, and you stand on tiptoe to look over the shoulders. Vines covered with flowers cascade down walls of whitewashed stone, and you see that you are in a small but pleasant courtyard.

"But, Ezekiel," says one man in a shocked voice. "We came to you today to comfort you. Why isn't your head bared in mourning?"

"How can you?" shouts a white-faced younger man. "Your wife was a lovely and gentle lady! How can you fail to mourn her?"

Your eyes are drawn to Ezekiel, bending over a large pot. His face is grey, and his mouth is a thin, grim line. His turban is neatly wound round his head, and nothing about his clothing suggests that he is in mourning for his dead wife. For one brief instant, he looks up—and waves of pity flood over you. His eyes hold unbearable grief. Then his gaze falls again to the contents of the pot, boiling fiercely over the fire.

"But the mourning feast!" wails the man next to you. "Our wives are busy now preparing the food. At least you will hold the mourning feast for your wife, Ezekiel!"

The prophet looks up. "No," he answers curtly. "There will be no feast of mourning."

Shocked gasps erupt all around you, and you can feel the crowd stiffen with disapproval. You ease your way through the crowd to stand finally only a few steps away from Ezekiel.

"Look at him!" snaps one. "He has filled that pot of boiling water with the choicest meats! The meat has all fallen off the bones—is that ridiculous stew more important than the death of your wife? You were boiling it yesterday, when your wife was still alive. Why are you doing that? What does it mean for us, prophet?"

Ezekiel calmly begins to remove pieces of meat

with a long-handled utensil, and throw them on the ground. You peer into the pot, and see that the water has all boiled away. The pot begins to scorch and glow red-hot, and still Ezekiel removes the contents, piece by piece.

Another man speaks, his voice throbbing with pity. "Ezekiel," he says softly. "Will you not tell us what these things that you are doing mean for us?"

The prophet looks up. "The word of the Lord came to me saying, 'Speak to the house of Israel, behold, I am about to profane My sanctuary, the pride of your power, the desire of your eyes, and the delight of your soul; and your sons and your daughters whom you have left behind will fall by the sword.'"

"The temple in Jerusalem!" whispers a man in the crowd. "Does this mean that the Lord's Temple will fall to Nebuchadnezzar's soldiers?"

Ezekiel's eyes flash now, as he faces the horrified group of men. "And you will do as I have done;" he says, his voice hoarse. "You will not cover your mustache, and you will not eat the bread of men. And your turbans will be on your heads and your shoes on your feet. You will not mourn, and you will not weep!"

The group drifts away swiftly, their faces white with shock. You are left alone with the prophet Ezekiel.

"Is it true?" you question softly. "Is God going to permit Nebuchadnezzar's soldiers to profane His temple in Jerusalem?"

Ezekiel's sorrowful eyes search your face. "On the very day that my wife died, Nebuchadnezzar began his final assault against Jerusalem. His soldiers will profane the Lord's temple, and the people of Jerusalem— rich and poor—will fall by the sword! The Lord will not mourn over Jerusalem's death, for His judgement has fallen upon her!"

You think for a moment, and then ask hesitantly, "But why do you not mourn your dead wife?"

Ezekiel sits heavily on a stone bench. "I do as the Lord commands me," he says simply. "She was the song of my life, and I loved her dearly."

Realization washes over you. *God commanded Ezekiel not to mourn his wife to show that God will not mourn the destruction of Jerusalem*! Shimmering flames engulf you, and you are once more in the chariot of fire.

"Here is your choice," says the steed. "I am allowed to take you to a beach where you will learn how Jonah survived being thrown overboard, or you may choose instead to visit the town on the Kebar where Ezekiel lives, almost two years in the future."

The voice falls silent, and you think carefully. Which path might help you more on your quest? Taking the reins absent-mindedly in your hands, you make your decision.

If you decide to find out how Jonah survived, go to page 18.

If you decide to go to the town in Babylon where Ezekiel lived, go to page 87.

(You Have Decided to See Ezekiel Taken to Babylon)

The press of bodies around you makes it difficult to breathe, and you notice with alarm that everyone is handcuffed. In front of you, a large metal cage is being carried along on men's shoulders. Inside the cage, a young man—you guess that he may be about eighteen or nineteen years old—is curled up on the floor, sobbing. "Who is that?" you whisper to the shackled man beside you.

He eyes you sadly. "Behold Jehoiachin, the king of Judah," he moans. "He did evil in the sight of the Lord just as his father before him. Again and again the Lord sent word to them by His messengers, because He had compassion on His people, but they continually mocked the messengers of God," he moans. "They despised His words and scoffed at His prophets. It is no wonder that all of Jerusalem is being led away captive!"

"All of Jerusalem?" you gasp in horror. "Is this the end of Jerusalem?"

Your companion shrugs. "No, young friend, not yet. There are still a few of my people who remain in our beloved city—although all our leading men and craftsmen are captives this day."

The woman on the other side of you jabs you sharply in the ribs. "Hush!" she hisses. "Do you think I want to listen to his whimpering?" Her dark eyes spark with hatred, as she continues, "We have more than six hundred miles to march, you old fool. I won't listen to your preaching all the way across the desert, I can promise you!"

A man marching in front turns to look at the woman, his face a strange mixture of sadness and triumph. "Do not reproach him, Hamutal," he says firmly. "He speaks only the truth, as you well know."

The woman tosses her head angrily. "Ezekiel the prophet!" she snorts furiously. "Now I suppose I will have to endure one of *your* messages."

Her harsh voice continues but you no longer hear her words. You find yourself staring at Ezekiel, led in handcuffs, bound for Babylon. You remember that Ezekiel *was* taken captive at the same time as the young king, Jehoiachin. Suddenly you stumble, and when you stand upright once more, you see that the rough road dips down before you. Gasping, you see thousands of shackled prisoners in the shimmering heat of the road that plunges sharply

into flat, barren desert. Then a blinding glare from heavily laden carts ahead pricks your eyes . "What is in those carts?" you mutter.

The old man moans, and Hamutal snorts. "Now you've set him off again!" she snaps. "The carts are filled with treasures from Jehoiachin's palace and the temple; plunder for the Babylonian king. Those riches never did *me* any good! Nebuchadnezzar can have them, for all I care!"

"Hey!" bellows a heavily-armed soldier, striding furiously toward you. "If you have enough energy to chatter, perhaps you all need some burdens to carry on this march!"

Hamutal begins to wail piteously, her thin cry rising to a grating whine. "No, please . . . may your gods have mercy on me. I am burdened enough with this old man's constant complaints!"

You gasp at her treachery, and you see the soldier's lips curl in a contemptuous smile. "I don't think that one poor, old man is burdening you overmuch, you old hag. Keep your tongue between your teeth from now on!" he orders crisply.

Sighing in relief, you watch the soldier move away. Your heart leaps in delight as you see the familiar flames of the chariot behind a projection of rock at the side of the road, and you push carefully through the press of bodies. Glancing around for a Babylonian soldier, you see none standing between you and the chariot, and you dart toward it.

You have one last glimpse of the thousands of Israelites marching miserably away from their home into captivity before the flames mercifully hide them from sight.

"Here is your choice," says the steed's calm voice. "You may go to the home of Ezekiel, some time after he has been taken to Babylon. Or you may see King Jehoiachin in captivity. On which destination will you decide?"

You find that you would truly like to see more of Ezekiel; but you are also curious about what happens to the young king. Taking the reins in your hands, you make your decision.

If you decide to go to Ezekiel's home, go to page 79.

If you decide to see King Jehoiachin, go to page 91.

(You Have Come to the Town in Babylon, Where Ezekiel Lives)

Sunshine sparkles off the surface of the water before you. Stripped to the waist and bent double, many men labor at the edges of the canal, dredging up loads of mud in wooden buckets. Behind you and on the other side of the canal, whitewashed one- and two-story houses dot the level landscape, each set like a jewel in a cultivated garden. A hard-packed dirt road separates the houses, and you notice in surprise that the sounds of dogs barking and children playing are much like the sounds of your own time.

"Come!" shouts a voice. "Let's hear the message from the Lord."

A group of men strides toward you down the dirt road, and you fall in silently behind them. The path leads between houses, and the men stop in front of a small, one-story house. The entry looms black in the sparkling white face of the house, and as you step into the shadowy entryway, you can see nothing.

"Ezekiel!" calls one of the men loudly.

Gradually, your eyes adjust to the dimness, and you follow the men out of the hall into the cool shade of the courtyard in the center of the small house. Several doors in each wall appear to lead off to other rooms, but your attention is drawn to a solitary figure sitting on a stone bench against the farthest wall. Crossing the brick court, the men bow respectfully and then seat themselves on the ground at the man's feet. You seat yourself quickly, watching the man intently.

From beneath dark brows jutting over piercing
black eyes, Ezekiel eyes the men before him.

"We have come to hear the Word of the Lord,
Ezekiel," stammers the oldest man. "Do you have a
message for us?"

Ezekiel stands, straightening his broad shoulders
until he looms above them. His eyes flash as he begins, "Thus says the Lord God, 'Behold, I am
against you, O Tyre, and I will bring up many nations against you, as the sea brings up its waves.
And they will destroy the walls of Tyre and break
down her towers; and I will scrape her debris from
her and make her a bare rock. She will be a place
for the spreading of nets in the midst of the sea, for
I have spoken,' declares the Lord God."

Startled gasps erupt from the men and they turn,

white with fear, toward Ezekiel. "How can this be?"

Ezekiel folds his arms calmly against his chest. "For thus says the Lord God," thunders Ezekiel, "'Behold, I will bring upon Tyre from the north Nebuchadnezzar king of Babylon, king of kings, with horses, chariots, cavalry, and a great army. He will slay your daughters on the mainland with the sword; and he will make siege walls against you!'"

The man next to you nods vigorously as he whispers to you, "If any ruler can defeat Tyre, it will be Nebuchadnezzar. I am not surprised that the Lord God is against Tyre!"

"Also," continues Ezekiel, "they will throw your stones and your timbers and your debris into the water. And the Lord God will make Tyre a bare rock; Tyre will be a place for the spreading of nets, and will be built no more, for the Lord has spoken!"

Shuddering, the men stand uneasily. "Is there no word for us, Ezekiel?" asks a younger man. "Will the Lord not end our captivity here in Babylon?"

Ezekiel meets his eyes with a level gaze. "You have heard how long we will be captive here," he says softly. "You know that we will be held for seventy years, for so the Lord God said. Do not ask what you already know!"

Seventy years! The answer burns in your brain for you already know that this prophecy also comes true!

Silently, the men cross the courtyard as Ezekiel turns abruptly on his heel and vanishes into the nearby doorway. The flames of your chariot glow in the tiny courtyard, and you climb aboard.

You realize that the prophecy about Tyre would mean more to you if you had any idea where it was. A gentle, faraway sound of tinkling chimes makes you wonder suddenly if your steed is laughing softly.

"Tyre was a city on the Mediterranean Sea, little one," says the voice quietly. "It was located north of Israel, in the country that is now called Lebanon."

You realize that the prophecy you have heard today was very clear, and very specific: God said that Nebuchadnezzar would destroy the mainland city of Tyre, that He would make her flat like the top of a rock, that fishermen would spread their nets there, and that debris from her destruction would be thrown into the water. You decide that you should be careful to remember these things, to see if they came true.

"Now I am allowed to take you into the future," the voice interrupts your thoughts. "You may decide to see Nebuchadnezzar destroy the mainland city of Tyre, or you may go much farther into the future to see Alexander the Great lay siege to Tyre. Which will you choose?"

Confused, you wonder why Alexander the Great laid siege to a city that had already been destroyed by Nebuchadnezzar. Or had it? You take the reins in your hands and make your decision.

If you decide to see Nebuchadnezzar destroy Tyre, go to page 95.

If you decide to see Alexander the Great, go to page 117.

(You Have Decided to
   See King Jehoiachin)

You look curiously around a spacious room, glowing softly now in the light of many oil lamps. A richly-colored rug covers the center of the smooth stone floor, and polished wooden chairs and tables are comfortably arranged in the pleasant room. You recognize the young man slumped in a chair as the very same person you had seen in the cage on the forced march from Jerusalem to Babylon.

"Well?" he snaps, as he lifts his head from his hands swiftly. "Your hands are empty! Are you deaf?" he sneers unpleasantly. "I told you to bring me wine—my head is throbbing!"

As you stand uncertainly, wondering what to do, an older woman sweeps past you, her rich robes swishing against the stone floor.

"Well, my king—another headache?" she asks coldly. "You have forgotten to sacrifice to Ashtoreth, or you would not be plagued with these headaches. No one here is preventing you from performing the proper attentions to the gods!"

Your scalp prickles uneasily. *The king of Judah surely would never sacrifice to a pagan idol!* You back carefully out of the room into the corridor, where a young man thrusts a tray toward you.

"Here!" he whispers. "You take his wine to him!" He whisks swiftly away down the corridor, and you walk back into the room. Crossing quietly to the gleaming table at the side of the king's chair, you place the decanter and goblet on it.

King Jehoiachin groans, gripping his head between

his hands. "I cannot live so!" he wails. "How can a king live captive in a strange land?!"

Glancing around the luxurious room, you reflect that this imprisonment doesn't seem so terrible. The older woman casts a contemptible glance over the miserable king, her lip curling in scorn.

"Weakling!" she snaps. Turning abruptly, she sweeps angrily from the room.

Summoning your courage, you ask softly, "Are you allowed to leave your house?"

The king raises his tortured face to yours. "Of course I may," he answers in surprise. "Nebuchadnezzar would never dare to limit my freedom!"

You think for a moment, and then ask, "Does he prevent you from worshiping God?"

"What has God done for me?" the king whines, leaping to his feet in irritation. He paces restlessly around the room. "My grandfather, old fool that he was, tore down and destroyed all the altars to the gods. He removed the mediums and the spiritists, and turned to the Lord with all his heart." Jehoiachin snorts angrily. "But my father was no fool! He saw to it that the altars to Baal were rebuilt, for who can risk offending any god?"

Creeping horror turns your blood to ice. "Your father sacrificed to Baal?" you whisper.

"Well, of course he did!" the king answers, staring at you curiously. "And he built altars for Baal and Ashtoreth in the temple in Jerusalem," he adds proudly.

Your jaw drops in astonishment. "In the Lord's temple?" you question. "He built altars to pagan gods in the Lord's temple that Solomon built?"

King Jehoiachin's brows draw together in an angry frown. "Enough!" he shrieks. "You weary me with your questions. Get out!"

Glad to obey, you almost run from the room. Leaning against the cool stone wall of the corridor you think, *How can he complain of his treatment in captivity?* you wonder. *He has a luxurious home, and is free to come and go as he pleases!* A brilliant white glow floods the empty corridor, and you scramble eagerly into the waiting chariot, happy to be leaving the self-pitying king.

The steed's voice floats musically in the pulsating silence of the dancing flames. "Now you must decide whether to go to a beach, where you will learn how Jonah survived being thrown overboard, or whether you wish to visit the town on the Kebar where Ezekiel lives, several years in the future."

I would like to know how Jonah managed to survive! you think in astonishment. You would also like to see the prophet Ezekiel again, but you have a feeling that you'll learn something from either choice you make. You pick up the cool leather reins, and pull them taut.

**If you decide to find out how
Jonah survived, go to page 18.**

**If you decide to go to the town in
Babylon where Ezekiel lived, go to page 87.**

(You Have Decided to See Nebuchadnezzar Destroy Tyre)

A terrible din assaults your ears as you find yourself in the midst of the Babylonian army at war. A hail of arrows whizzes past you, coming from inside the massive walls in front of you. You stumble over a shield on the ground and glance swiftly around. Stooping quickly, you pick it up. Grim-faced soldiers rush past you, heavy maces and swords gripped tightly in their hands.

"Here, you!" bellows a voice in your ear. "We'll need an extra body on the battering ram!"

He propels you mercilessly forward, shoving you toward a massive battering ram. You quickly grab a vacant handle—seemingly made from a metal spike pounded into the huge tree trunk. The ram is mounted on a wagon. Over the ram, a shielded tower holds an archer who is busily engaged in releasing one arrow after another over the city gates before you.

"We're almost in!" shouts a soldier as he grins broadly. "Tyre will be ours!"

You heave with the rest as the massive battering ram strikes the wooden gates with a shudder. The sound of splintering wood is unmistakable and suddenly, the ram surges forward—the resistance of the gates is no more. Bloodthirsty yells erupt from everyone around you and the soldiers leap away from the battering ram, their swords ringing as they draw them from their scabbards and rush toward the gaping hole where once the gates of Tyre had stood.

Black smoke rises from almost every building,

and as you enter, you can see from the crumbling and blackened buildings that terrible damage has already been inflicted on this once-proud city. An older soldier, his face lined with the scars of many battles, slumps wearily against the inside of the city wall. Hesitantly, you approach him—wondering if he has been wounded.

"Are you hurt?" you ask quietly.

His eyes fly open at your words, and he smiles wanly. "No, youngster," he replies. "Just tired. I'm too old to enjoy the taste for battle anymore.

Besides," he sighs, "thirteen years is a long time to besiege a city—and I don't think that we'll find anyone left in Tyre to fight!"

"Thirteen years!" you exclaim. "Is everyone dead by now?"

The old soldier shakes his head. "No, not dead. They have been busy moving by ship to the island half a mile off the coast. We'll destroy this city—but Nebuchadnezzar will never be able to destroy the island city of Tyre!"

As you look around at the crumbling, burning ruins, you know that this city will indeed be destroyed—and you remember Ezekiel's prophecy that Nebuchadnezzar would destroy the *mainland* city of Tyre. Babylonian soldiers shout in delight from the towers as they begin tearing them apart, stone by stone. The old soldier smiles briefly, and turns to you.

"Leave this place, youngster," he says gently. "This city is dead, and will rise no more."

"But how do you know it will never be built again?" you ask curiously.

A smile lights his face for one fleeting instant. "Because the God of the Hebrew captives has said so," he answers simply. "I have a friend who is chief official to King Nebuchadnezzar himself," he continues, the smile still warm in his eyes. "We've known each other since boyhood—and if there is anyone more bull-headed than Ashpenaz, I'd like to meet him!" His shoulders shake with laughter. "He has been in charge of some Hebrew nobles, and he has seen what marvels their God can perform!"

The old soldier looks around cautiously. "More than sixteen years ago my old friend Ashpenaz told me about a Hebrew prophet by the name of Ezekiel. He didn't know the prophet personally, but he had heard that Ezekiel had predicted the fall of Tyre!"

A chariot rumbles through the gate and the old soldier straightens quickly. The chariot halts, its horses rearing and foaming, and a heavily-armed soldier leaps to the ground and strides toward your companion.

"Here you are, you old buzzard!" laughs the

young soldier, looking fondly at the older man. "Come! Get up in the chariot with me and rest your old legs for a while!"

Together they mount behind the horses, and the sight of the burning city is blotted out by the flames of your own chariot. The steed's musical voice chimes bell-like in your ears.

"Your choice now is between two times," says the steed. "I may take you to this same place in your own time, or you may go backward in time. I would strongly recommend the first choice."

You realize that you are learning so much from the past that you feel reluctant to visit your own time. *What could I possibly learn from visiting Tyre again in the twentieth century?* you reflect. Or should you listen to the steed's advice? You pick up the reins, and make the decision hastily.

If you decide to go to Tyre in the 20th century, go to page 134.

If you decide to go back in time, go to page 17.

(You Have Decided to Join the Merchant on His Way to Petra)

The scorched landscape sizzles under a blistering sun, and craggy red mountains jut up from the flat grey plain. A soft, moist touch on the back of your elbow startles you, and you turn to see a gentle-eyed donkey regarding you hopefully.

"She knows we are almost there!" says a voice with a chuckle, "and she wants to remind you to feed her once we get to Petra!"

You turn to see a prosperous.looking man leading a caravan of several donkeys. Enormous straw baskets hang over their backs, filled with brilliantly-colored, shimmering cloth. You know that he is on his way to Petra, but you decide that it must be miles away, for you can see nothing but the rosy cliffs and flat grey earth.

"Almost there?" you ask in surprise. "Is Petra beyond those mountains?"

The merchant's dark eyes twinkle and he throws back his head in delighted laughter. "Ho!" he roars "You've never been to Petra, I can see that!" His shoulders shaking with mirth, he continues, "See that narrow, dry riverbed coming up?"

You see the flat wadi ahead of you, sloping gradually downward, and you nod.

"Follow it, my friend—and we shall be in Petra in less than half an hour!"

You wonder briefly if the merchant is a bit crazy, but since you have never heard of Petra anyway . . . "What is Petra, exactly?" you ask hesitantly.

The man smiles. "You *are* ignorant, my friend!"

he replies, but the kindness on his face takes the sting out of his words. "Petra is the capital of the ancient land of Edom. Jacob's brother Esau was the founder of the Edomites, and Esau's hatred of Jacob was passed from generation to generation," he adds, shuddering slightly.

"After Moses led the Hebrews out of Egypt, they asked permission to travel through Edom on the King's Highway. It would have been a much faster route to Canaan, but the ruler of Edom refused. To make a long history short," he says briskly, "Edom has always been an enemy to Israel. And so, when Nebuchadnezzar of Babylon attacked Judah and carried the Hebrews into captivity, the Edomites rejoiced over Judah's misfortune! They even helped in the plundering and killing! That is why God gave Isaiah the prophecy against Edom," he finishes solemnly.

Electrified, you ask eagerly, "Do you know the prophecy?"

"I love the Word of the Lord God," answers the man softly. "How could I not know the prophecy?"

You glance around, and see that as you have been walking, the riverbed has become a deep ravine, with high and straight walls impossible to climb. Still it plunges downward, and the towering sides shade you from the hot sun overhead.

The merchant's gaze is faraway. "The Lord has said through His prophet Isaiah that none shall pass through Petra; and that it will become a desolation which wild animals will inhabit."

"That has happened already, hasn't it?" you reply in excitement.

"No, not yet, but it will!" your companion replies slowly. "Petra stands on one of the greatest trade routes in the world, my friend. Through this great city come spices and silks from the orient bound for mighty Rome. But the Lord has said that Petra will become a desolation, and all His promises are true. He has said that trade will cease, and that only wild animals will inhabit the site. It will come to pass, someday, exactly as He has said!"

The ravine has narrowed suddenly to approximately eight feet in width. Rocky cliffs tower hundreds of feet above, and as you round a sharp bend, you freeze in total amazement at what you see.

Graceful pillars soar to the roofs of massive rose-red buildings, all cut out of the rock cliffs. Richly-robed men and women bustle back and forth between buildings that are every bit as splendid as the most beautiful buildings of Washington, D.C. The entire city seems to be carved from the surrounding cliffs, and it is difficult to imagine that such a busy city could ever become a desolation.

A babble of voices haggle over prices, different languages tumbling into each other and breaking apart into a thousand splinters of sound. The merchant chuckles as he watches you.

The scene disappears as the flames of the chariot engulf you. You are so amazed that you almost fail to hear the soft voice of your steed.

"Mark well what you have seen," it says. "Now I shall take you to Petra today."

Your thoughts reeling, you wait expectantly.

Go to page 139.

(You Have Come to See the Fall of Jerusalem)

Leaping flames surround you still, and the voice of the steed is stern. "Behold, you are in the temple of the Lord in Jerusalem. Mark well what you see!"

As the flames disappear, you stand awed in the magnificent temple built by Solomon. Shrieks echo eerily from beyond huge bronze doors guarding the entrance of the temple, and several women kneel in the courtyard, weeping. You touch one young woman on the shoulder, your heart wrung by sympathy.

"You weep for Jerusalem, don't you?" you ask gently. The woman turns a blank face toward you, tears still spilling out of her swollen eyes. "Jerusalem?" she repeats dully. "No, of course not! I weep for Tammuz!"

"Tammuz?" you question, mystified. "Who is that?" The young woman's eyes narrow suspiciously. "He is the slain son of the goddess, Semerimus, of course. We are mourning his death until he rises from the dead in forty days!"

The hairs on the back of your neck prickle. *This woman mourns a pagan deity in the very courtyard of the temple of the Lord!* She rushes into speech eagerly now. "Then, after forty days, we may hold our glorious feast of Ishtar. Surely you have seen the beautiful colored eggs we exchange to rejoice over the resurrection of Tammuz?"

Horrified, you back away from the group of women, returning to the court of the priests at your

back. A series of chambers line the sides of the long room, and you enter the nearest chamber timidly.

In growing revulsion, you see that niches have been carved in the walls and in each recess stands a pagan idol! Several men, their lips moving soundlessly, stand before the altars waving a censer of incense rhythmically back and forth. *How dare they?* your mind shrieks in horror. *In the temple of the Lord they are worshiping pagan idols!*

You back out of the room, for you have seen

enough. Your stomach churns as you race across the courtyard of the temple. The rumble of advancing soldiers dimly penetrates your brain and you look up in surprise to see thick smoke rolling down the street toward you, and sheets of flame reaching into the sky. Black plumes of smoke curl from buildings, and the clang of swords mixes horribly with screams of terror.

A white-faced boy races toward you. "Run!" he shrieks, his chest heaving. "The Babylonians have breached the walls; Jerusalem is doomed!" He tugs impatiently at your arm, then races away.

You stand in the middle of the street, your thoughts tumbling over each other. Overcome by the awfulness of the blasphemy you have witnessed in the temple, and the terror of the advancing army, you sink to your knees. You wonder if you will ever feel clean or safe again. Suddenly, the pure white flames of the chariot of fire surround you like a warm, protective blanket.

"Sin defiles, little one," speaks the steed gently. "But if you are Christian, you are cleansed already."

Gratefully you sink back against the solid side of the chariot; you will be glad to get away from here!

"Now I shall take you more than seventy years forward in time, where you will learn from the prophet Zechariah. Your quest is almost finished," the steed says softly.

Torn between excitement and reluctance, you take the cool leather reins into your hands and wait.

Go to page 113.

(You Have Decided to See the Fall of Babylon)

You are standing at the back of an enormous room. The walls are constructed of colored bricks, some of which extend from the deep blue background in the shapes of yellow lions and red, yellow, and blue columns. A long banquet table commands the center of the room, and your eyes widen at the profusion of golden goblets and platters piled upon the wooden table. Spilled wine drips slowly to the floor, unheeded by the men who slump drunkenly over their golden platters. Coarse laughter echoes off the high ceilings, and you see the man at the head of the table stagger drunkenly to his feet. *He must be the king*! you reflect in disgust, as you notice that his crown has slipped crazily over one eye.

A soldier strides swiftly into the room, his mouth a disapproving straight line. "My king!" he says, bowing deeply. "You are in danger. Babylon is falling!"

The king giggles stupidly, raising his goblet high in the air. "0 noble soldier! Will you join me in a drink of celebration to the great god, Marduk?"

Frowning, the soldier repeats, "Babylon is falling, my king! You are in danger!"

The king's eyes fix intently on the goblet he holds in his hand. Slowly, he turns it this way and that, and at last his lips spread into a wicked smile. "These little items my family's soldiers took from the temple in Jerusalem are pretty trinkets, are they not? I can put them to much better use than the Israelites ever did!" he sneers, as he raises the

goblet to his lips and downs its contents greedily.

The soldier bows stiffly, his eyes angry. Swift strides take him away from the banquet table, where no man has comprehended his message. He looks at you, and beckons curtly. "Come! You are in terrible danger here," he says.

You follow him out of the hall at a trot, and find that you must jog to stay by his side through the wide deserted hallway.

"How do you know for certain that Babylon is falling?" you question nervously.

The soldier snorts contemptuously. "I have seen with my own eyes what the Persian army has been doing—but my superiors only laugh at me, and drink to their useless god, Marduk! You know that the mighty Euphrates river runs beneath our city walls. The Persians have dug canals to divert the River Euphrates!"

You frown over this, puzzled. "How will digging canals help them to attack Babylon?"

"That is exactly what my superiors have asked!" he explodes. "I would not expect you to understand," he says, a smile softening his harsh words, "for you are not trained in the art of warfare. But they are! Here is what will happen: They have dug canals and built dams in order to divert the river. When they are finished, they will be able to march an army through the dry river bed, under our walls, and straight into Babylon!"

"Oh!" you cry, as this information sinks in.

"Exactly!" he answers, his mouth grim. "Not only that, but two men from our own army, Gobryas and Gadatas, have deserted to the Persians. They will be able to inform the Persian army about where our defenses are positioned, the plan of the city—everything! Babylon is finished. It is only a matter of time now!"

The soldier turns to you. "I must go, and you must get out of the city. Stay on the narrow back streets, and hurry!" He takes your hand in a firm, brief handclasp, then strides off down broad steps.

A bright glow of light illuminates the hall, and you turn to see the chariot of fire behind you. You climb thoughtfully in behind the steed. "I am allowed to take you now to the court of Cyrus the Great, where you may hear Isaiah's prophecy fulfilled as Cyrus issues the decree that will allow the Hebrew people to return to Jerusalem and rebuild the temple."

Eagerly you wait.

Go to page 111.

(You Have Come to Hear Cyrus Issue the Decree)

For an instant, the leaping flames blot everything from your sight. Then they disappear and you find yourself in an enormous room. Marble columns support the lofty ceiling, and the polished floor glows. Richly-robed men, their tall, pleated hats bright and distinctive, cluster in groups at the foot of the dais at the front of the room.

"Do you think he really will allow us to go back to Israel?" a woman whispers. You turn to see a knot of people watching the king on the dais. The liquid brown eyes of the woman who spoke are fixed with painful intensity on Cyrus, her hands clasping and unclasping in anguish.

Cyrus the Great stands suddenly, and a scribe kneeling at the foot of the dais holds his stylus poised expectantly over a wet clay cylinder. All conversation dies and the room is hushed as every eye fastens on the king of Persia.

"The Lord, the God of Heaven, has given me all the kingdoms of the earth," he pronounces slowly, "and He has appointed me to build Him a house in Jerusalem, which is in Judah."

Startled gasps erupt from the little knot of people behind you, and you cast a swift glance at the young woman.

"Whosoever there is among you of all His people, may his God be with him! Let him go up to Jerusalem and rebuild the house of the Lord."

"Praise be to the Lord most high!" the woman sings out joyfully. "We may go home! After seventy

years in captivity, we may go home and rebuild the Lord's temple!"

The flames of the chariot engulf you once more as the voice of the steed sounds low in your ears. "I am allowed to take you more than fifty years backward in time to hear the prophet Ezekiel predict the fall of Jerusalem, or I may take you almost twenty years into the future to hear the prophecies of Zechariah. What is your decision?"

Backward, or forward in time? You wonder which would be the best decision. You don't have any idea, so you take the reins in your hands and make your choice hastily.

**If you decide to go back
to Ezekiel's prophecy, go to page 66.**

**If you decide to go forward
to Zechariah's prophecy, go to page 113.**

(You Have Come to Hear Zechariah's Prophecy)

Low, whitewashed houses straggle uphill from encircling walls, and dogs and children tumble in play in the dusty streets. A bent, old man, struggles toward the nearest house, where a solitary figure sits on a rough wooden bench. His white hair forms a halo of light in the bright sunlight as he heaves himself with a groan of relief onto the bench.

"Oh, Zechariah!" he sighs wearily. "It pains me every time I go to this poor excuse of a temple we have built. I was just a little boy when Jerusalem was destroyed and we were taken captive to Babylon—but I still remember the glorious temple of Solomon!" He sighs gustily once more, and continues, "I am grateful that we were allowed to return home, of course, but I miss the old temple!" A tear squeezes out of the corner of his eye, and he dashes it away furtively with the back of his hand.

Zechariah smiles at the old man. "Old friend," he says gently, "Do not be sad."

The old man's face brightens. "Tell me again, Zechariah! Tell me the word of the Lord that begins, 'Rejoice greatly...' I keep forgetting how the whole thing goes."

The prophet stands and looks directly at you. He motions you kindly to join the old man, and you lean contentedly against the warm stone wall of the house.

"Listen to this, youngster," the old man's eyes twinkle happily as he smiles at you.

"Rejoice greatly, O Daughter of Zion! Shout, Daughter of Jerusalem! See, your king comes to you, righteous and having salvation, gentle and riding on a donkey, on a colt, the foal of a donkey."* You sit straight up in astonishment. *Five hundred years before Christ was born, Zechariah has prophesied that He will enter Jerusalem riding on a donkey!*

You summon your courage, and ask, "That prophecy is about the Messiah, isn't it?"

Zechariah's eyes meet yours levelly. "Yes, my friend."

You take a deep breath, and continue. "Has God given you other prophecies about the Messiah?"

The prophet's face clouds suddenly, and a spasm of pain twists his mouth. "The Lord appointed me as a shepherd over the people, and gave them many opportunities to follow my leading. But the people continued to go their own way until the Lord allowed many of them to perish. Those who were watching knew that this was punishment from God. Still, when I asked whether or not they valued my leadership, the people paid thirty shekels of silver as my wages. This amount was insulting to the Lord and He said to me, 'Throw it to the potter — the handsome price at which they priced me!' So I took the thirty pieces of silver and threw them into the house of the Lord to the potter ."

You gasp, and for an instant the world around you seems to reel crazily. You know that thirty pieces of silver was the amount that Judas was given in exchange for betraying Jesus! And, that after Judas

---

*Zechariah 9:9

threw the money into the temple, the priests decided they could not return blood money to the treasury, so they used it to buy a potter's field!

Zechariah's eyes never leave your face as he continues, "And the Lord has said that He will pour out on the house of David and on the inhabitants of Jerusalem, a spirit of grace and of supplication. And the people will look on God, whom they have pierced, and they will mourn for Him as one mourns for an only child, and grieve bitterly for Him as one grieves for a firstborn son. On that day the weeping in Jerusalem will be great."

Your thoughts whirl feverishly, as you reflect in awe that you have just heard *six* prophecies: The Messiah will enter Jerusalem on a donkey. He will be sold for thirty pieces of silver. The money will be thrown to a potter by way of the temple. The Messiah will be pierced. Jerusalem will recognize Him as the Son of God, and will grieve over what has been done.

Flames dance around you as Zechariah and his companion disappear. "Your choice now is between the future and the past," chimes the voice. "You may go forward to the temple of the Lord in Jerusalem at the very time of Christ's betrayal; or you may go back to the time of Isaiah to meet the prophet Micah. The choice is yours."

Awed, you make your decision swiftly.

If you decide to meet the prophet Micah,
go to page 62.

If you decide to go to the temple
in Jerusalem, go to page 122.

(You Have Decided to See Alexander the Great)

You clap your hands over your ears as the deafening roar of a battle shakes the very floor on which you are standing. You are next to a slit of a window, and you press your face against the rough wood frame to peer through. You are looking down from the height of a twenty-story tower—so tall and so narrow that you wonder how it can stand. All around the base, men are fighting. In the distance the sea is crowded with ships—many of them sinking in flames. Mighty stone walls have crumbled into ruins, and Greek soldiers clamber over the debris, their swords flashing in the sun.

"How did *you* get up here?" growls a voice in your ear.

Startled, you wheel around to confront a Greek soldier.

He scowls briefly, and then sighs. "I guess it won't matter now," he says. "The battle is won at last—Tyre is finished! And we have taken this mighty fortification in only seven months! Come," says the soldier. "We have no need of this siege tower now. Let's go down."

Together you climb down the ladder set in the center of the tower, passing level after level on your way—each with slits from which to shoot arrows. As you emerge from the shadowy siege tower, your eyes suddenly narrow against the glare of sunlight sparkling on the water.

You find that you are standing on a broad, level peninsula. In one direction you can see the now

crumbling walls of the island city of Tyre—and in the other direction, the mainland. You remember that Ezekiel predicted that Nebuchadnezzar would destroy the *mainland* city of Tyre, and you squint into the distance, looking for the remains of the great mainland city.

The soldier beside you chuckles. "Imagine! One of the most powerful cities in the world once stood there," he muses. "Nothing remains of it now. Our general swept it clean!"

Electrified, you ask swiftly, "Who destroyed the mainland city? Was it Alexander the Great?"

The soldier looks at you strangely. "You must have been living in a cave, youngster!" he replies. "No, my general did not destroy the mainland city. That was accomplished by Nebuchadnezzar, the famous Babylonian king! But the fortified island city was too strong for a king with no ships. The island city of Tyre has fallen to the mightiest general the world has ever seen—Alexander!"

You look at the broad spit of land leading to the crumbling city in the sea. "Why would Nebuchadnezzar have needed ships to take the city?" you ask, puzzled. "He could have just marched his soldiers from the mainland out to the island city on this peninsula!"

The soldier's shoulders shake with laughter. "Ho!" he roars. "This peninsula wasn't here until *we* built it!"

"Your army built this?" you gasp, looking in amazement at the two-hundred-foot-wide spit of land, at least half a mile in length.

"Stone by stone, youngster!" the soldier replies grimly. "Every stone left of the old mainland city of Tyre was thrown into the water to make this spit of land!"

Excitement races through you, as you realize that this is an *exact fulfullment of prophecy*! Ezekiel's words seem to ring in your ears: "They will throw your stones and your timbers and your debris into the water!"—*exactly* what has been done by the army of Alexander the Great *more than two hundred years after the prophecy!*

"It's strange, too," murmurs the soldier as he gazes over the sparkling water. "Usually, after a city is destroyed—as Tyre was by Nebuchadnezzar—the stones are used by others to build other cities. I've never known of stones and pillars to be left lying in place for over two hundred years! Most unusual!" he murmurs, shaking his head.

He gives you a friendly pat on the back. "I must be off. Do not come to the island city, youngster—we are not quite finished there, although the battle has been won." With a wave of farewell, the soldier jogs down the spit of land toward the island city. Sea birds wheel overhead, and you take one last look at the mainland—scraped flat and level—before the flames engulf you.

"Have you learned something important?" asks the musical voice gently.

Still amazed, you answer slowly, "The prophecy of Ezekiel came true exactly!" you marvel.

The soft tinkling of distant bells sparkles in the air around you. "You are amazed that the Word of the Lord is true, little one? But it is time for your decision. You may go to Tyre in your own time; but keep in mind that the town called Tyre in Lebanon is not built on exactly the same site as the old mainland city of Tyre. Or you may go back in time—but I would recommend the first choice."

You take the reins hurriedly in your hands and make the decision.

**If you decide to go to Tyre today,
go to page 134.**

**If you decide to go back in time,
go to page 17.**

(You Have Come to
   the Temple in Jerusalem)

The faraway cry of a rooster announces morning.
The sun has not yet warmed the long, cold stone
porch on which you find yourself. You shiver a little in the damp early-morning air, and peer beyond
the columns into the enormous courtyard beyond.
The temple towers into the sky behind sheltering
walls, its bronze columns blood-red as they catch
the first brilliant rays of sun. A solitary man races
across the paved courtyard and into the sheltering
portico where you are; his face is full of anguish
and his beard flecked with foam. Casting quick
glances over his shoulder, he makes for a group of
men standing in the deep shadows of the columned
portico.

"I have sinned," he rasps, as he tugs on the sleeve
of one of the men. The man withdraws a step, his
lip curling scornfully. You have a feeling that these

men must be high priests of Israel, for you recognize the tall cloth headgear. Your stomach churns as you watch the miserable man, for you know that he must be Judas Iscariot.

He speaks again, his voice hoarse. "I have sinned by betraying innocent blood."

One of the high priests casts a contemptuous glance at Judas. "What is that to us?" he answers, with a careless shrug.

With trembling hands, Judas removes a cloth pouch from his tunic, and empties silver coins into his hand. A cry seems torn from his throat as the silver spills into his hand, and he flings the coins upon the ground at the feet of the priests. Whirling around, he runs madly across the courtyard, and out of sight. You have only one brief glimpse of his eyes as he races past you—and one glance is enough. You see only terror.

One of the priests motions curtly to you. "Pick up the coins, youngster," he commands tonelessly.

You draw near and drop to your knees on the chilly stone, counting the silver coins as you collect them. The priests cluster uneasily together, heedless of you at their feet.

"What shall we do with this?" snarls one. "It is the price Judas agreed on, after all!"

"He earned his money," replies another, his voice cold. "He came to us. We did not seek him out. There is no blood on *our* hands!"

Your heart pounds in your ears and the world begins to spin crazily, for you have picked up the last piece of silver, and have counted to thirty. *That is the exact price prophesied by Zechariah—and there is absolutely no way that this could be chance*! you reflect. Hurriedly, you stand on weak knees, holding your hands out to the high priests.

A priest looks at the coins in disgust, his nostrils flaring. "It is not lawful to put this money back into the temple treasury," he says slowly, "since it is blood money."

Still you stand, holding the coins in your unwilling hands, as the priests discuss what they will do with it. At last one priests throws his hands into the air in a gesture of irritation and impatience. "Come, let us make an end of this discussion!" he snaps, as he scoops the coins out of your hands. "We will buy a piece of land with these thirty pieces of silver to be used as a burial place for strangers."

The priests nod in agreement, and one says casually, "I know of such a piece of ground. There is a field not far from here which is good for nothing but a burial place. It has been used by a potter to draw his clay and the land is no good for farming. It will do to bury strangers in."

They hurry away toward the temple, leaving you standing there thunderstruck. You have *counted* thirty pieces of silver—the price of betrayal of the Messiah. You have *seen* it thrown to the priests in the courtyard of the house of the Lord, and now they will throw it to a potter—*exactly* as foretold hundreds of years before by the prophet Zechariah!

The musical voice of the steed chimes softly through the shimmering flames that now hide the magnificent temple from your sight. "Now you shall go a very few days into the future, to speak with someone who has actually seen the risen Lord."

Shaking with anticipation, you take up the reins.

Go to page 126.

(You Have Come to Meet Someone Who Has Seen the Risen Lord)

A strong hand grips your arm painfully, pulling you behind a large boulder. You face a young man, whose finger is placed warningly over his lips as he nods in the direction of a dusty road. Sunlight flashes off the burnished shields of well-armed soldiers, marching in formation.

"Shh!" the young man cautions in a whisper. "The Romans have been more aggressive than usual lately. They wouldn't appreciate our being here!"

You glance curiously at your surroundings, and feel a surge of excitement. Flowers bloom in riotous confusion, cascading down a gentle hill jutting over a sheer rock face. A huge dark opening yawns in the middle of the flat rock wall, and a deep trench has been cut from the rock floor in front of the cave mouth. A massive stone disk, fitting snugly inside the trench, has been rolled away from the opening, and you can see that the disk would completely hide the cave mouth.

"Is that . . . " you trail off, pointing with trembling hand toward the opening.

The young man nods, his eyes wide with awe. "Yes, that is the tomb of Jesus, the Messiah!" he answers. "Is this the first time you have come here?"

You nod wordlessly, hearing as if from a great distance the trill of birds, and the hushed whisper of leaves in the still garden.

The young man's face floods with excitement and joy. "I come here every day," he says, no longer whispering as the tramp of soldiers' feet recedes into the distance. "I saw Him, you know," he adds in awe.

"Tell me," you say simply.

He shakes his head wonderingly. "My family saw Him heal my uncle—he was a leper. After that, you can imagine that we went to hear Him teach every chance we had! My father told me about all the prophecies," the young man's dark eyes sparkle with excitement. "The Messiah was to be born in Bethlehem, He was to enter Jerusalem on a donkey; the prophet Isaiah foretold so many things—and *all* were fulfilled by Jesus!"

Eagerly you ask, "What did Isaiah foretell?"

The young man rushes into speech, his words tumbling over each other. "That the Messiah would be born of a virgin, that He would be worshiped by wise men and presented with gifts, that He would heal many, that He would speak in parables, that He would be rejected by His own, and that He would be scourged and spat upon."

You remember all the prophecies that you have seen fulfilled with your own eyes, and marvel.

The young man gazes at the empty tomb before you. "I was so sure that Jesus was the Messiah," he says. "Then when the Romans crucified Him . . . " his voice falls low, "I thought all was lost. *Then* my father heard that the tomb was empty!"

"But wait," you begin slowly. "Didn't many people believe that Jesus' body had been stolen?"

"Stolen!" he snorts scornfully. "Under the noses of a full Roman guard of sixteen soldiers? Not likely!"

"Could the soldiers have been asleep?" you ask.

The young man doubles over in laughter. "No, my friend they couldn't have been! A Roman soldier is executed if he falls asleep on post. They couldn't have become rulers of the known world if they were lax in discipline. And no one could sneak in and just push that stone away — you can see the size of it! How many men do you think it would take to get that stone to budge one inch?" You stare

at the massive stone disk in amazement. You had never imagined that it would be so large.

"But the very best part," the young man continues, "is that *I saw the risen Lord!*" His voice throbs with adoration. "My family came to see the empty tomb, to make sure with our own eyes that He was not there. After His death, we wept, for we were all sick at heart—we had been so certain that He was the Messiah. But then we came and saw the empty tomb, and *then*—we saw *Him!*

You lean forward eagerly, chills of excitement washing over you.

"We had left the tomb and were on the road home, when—*there He was*! He looked at us with such love and compassion, and we knew that we were not mistaken: Jesus Christ was and *is* the One spoken of by the prophets! While we were yet sinners, Christ died for us. He was buried, He was raised on the third day according to the Scriptures! *He lives*!!!"

Tears fill your eyes as the young man's radiant face disappears in the leaping flames of the chariot. From your vantage point in time, you have long believed that Jesus was—and is—the Son of God, but how magnificent it has been to talk to one who saw Jesus perform a miracle and see Him alive after He was killed! You realize with a pang of regret that this quest is over, but your sorrow turns to joy when you remember that the larger adventure of living in Jesus has only just begun!

THE END

(You Have Decided to Go to the Archaeological Dig)

You blink in surprise at your surroundings—you are standing in the shadow of an oddly-shaped hill that looms overhead. Somehow, the hill looks out of place in the flat plain stretching toward the mountains in the distance. On the hill, workmen labor toward the summit, pick-axes over their shoulders. Around the base, several tents huddle against the fierce blasts of hot wind. A tall, thin man bursts from the largest tent and motions to you excitedly.

"Ah, my friend, you have come at the perfect time," he says jubilantly. "Now let them laugh at Sir Austen Layard!" The man grasps your wrist with surprising strength, and lopes toward the base of the hill.

Your chest heaving, you and Sir Austen Layard reach the summit. His cheeks flushed and his eyes sparkling with excitement, the man sweeps off his pith helmet and gestures expansively. "Behold Nineveh!" he exclaims grandly.

Your jaw drops as you survey the hill—you see no city of antiquity here, only a mound rising strangely from the level plain. "Here?" you question, trying not to sound disbelieving.

A smile quivers briefly on Sir Austen's face. "Ho!" he laughs gently. "Another skeptic! This mound, I am convinced, covers the ruins of Nineveh. Just think!" he cries, his clipped British accent slurring a bit in excitement. "Napoleon and his army traveled past this very spot, never

imagining that they marched past the walls of one of the mightiest cities of the ancient world!"

You gaze in awe at the stark hill, and suddenly you remember Nahum's prophecy against Nineveh: "She will be total desolation and waste." "Nahum was right," you murmur.

Sir Austen nods vigorously. "Oh yes, my friend — he was right! Nineveh fell so completely that even a short two hundred years after her fall, the Greek general Xenophon saw only desolate ruins. And now," he continues, a delighted grin playing over his face, "after being buried for more than two thousand years, Nineveh will give us her secrets!"

The hair on the back of your neck prickles as you realize that you have seen with your own eyes that one part of Nahum's prophecy was literally

fulfilled. *How many other prophecies have come to pass too?* you reflect in awe.

Sir Austen claps his pith helmet upon his head, and almost gallops toward a workman who is examining the contents of his shovel in surprise. As you glance down at the plain below, you see the chariot of fire waiting. Half running and half sliding, you scramble down the desolate mound which was Nineveh.

As you clamber in behind the steed, the blasts of gusting wind dissolve into the throbbing silence of the flames. "Now you shall see the fall of Nineveh," says the steed solemnly.

Here we go! you think in excitement.

Go to page 73.

(You Have Decided to Go to Tyre Today)

Fleecy clouds drift lazily in the deep-blue sky overhead and the gulls scold noisily. You are standing on a quay overlooking the Mediterranean Sea, and the waves slosh gently against the stone beneath your feet. Flat, whitewashed buildings cluster behind you, and the orange tiles of a church steeple reach into the sky. The industry here is unmistakable: the sea is crowded with small fishing boats and the smell of fish is overpowering!

You begin to stroll along the quay, looking down into the shallow water at the waterfront's edge. You stop suddenly, staring into the water. Excited, you drop to your hands and knees—for you are certain that you catch a glimpse of a massive stone pillar beneath the waves!

"Looking for Tyre?" an amused voice above you asks.

A woman stoops easily to join you, her deeply-tanned face a network of tiny wrinkles. Twinkling blue eyes meet yours as the woman's smile lights up her face.

"I thought I saw a column underwater," you begin uncertainly.

A delighted laugh escapes the woman. "Sharp eyes! Good for you!" she says approvingly. "Yes indeed, you do see a column. And if you look even more carefully," she continues, as she lies flat on her stomach on the quay, "you can even see the huge granite building blocks of the old mainland city of Tyre!"

You follow her example, and both of you peer over the edge of the quay into the water below. Gradually, as your eyes grow accustomed to the shifting patterns of light and shadow beneath, you begin to recognize the outlines of the building blocks — flung there by the hands of Alexander's soldiers more than two thousand years ago!

With a sigh of satisfaction, the woman stands. "I never tire of looking," she says dreamily, "but it is better to share the sight with someone."

You scramble to your feet, and the woman's brilliant smile floods her face again. "Look!" she says happily, raising her arm to point in the direction of a wide peninsula of land reaching out into the sea.

Pale blue fishing nets are spread out to dry on the shore, and suddenly you remember. "She will be a place for the spreading of nets in the midst of the sea!" you shout, with Ezekiel's words ringing in your ears.

"Ah!" the woman breathes. "So you know about the prophet Ezekiel!" Her face shines raptly, as she continues, "I do not understand how anyone can mock the prophets — all they have to do is *look*! Everything that Ezekiel prophesied came to pass. Think of it!" Her words tumble out in excitement now, and the two of you walk companionably along the quay.

"Nebuchadnezzar destroyed the mainland city of Tyre," she says, counting off on the fingers of her hand. "Alexander the Great scraped the old site clean, making it like a bare rock — in order to build the causeway out to the island city. He threw the stones and timbers of Tyre into the sea to form a

base for the causeway," she pauses for breath, then continues, "and as you said, where the proud city once stood is now a place for the spreading of nets in the midst of the sea! All *exactly* as predicted!" she finishes triumphantly.

This is truly amazing! you reflect in astonishment. You remember your quest, and know that you are learning. "Were the other prophets as accurate as Ezekiel?" you ask.

The woman smiles gently. "You have much to learn," she says softly, "as I once did. Many years ago, I felt that the Bible was a collection of myths and fairy tales—not something to be believed by a person as educated as I!" she laughs merrily. "But what is intelligence? she asks.

"Well," you begin slowly, "I think that an intelligent person is always open-minded, and looks for evidence that proves a fact to be true."

"Exactly!" she replies. "I prided myself on my intellect—and so I decided that instead of *assuming* that the Bible was myth, I should explore the facts myself. I began with the prophecies of Ezekiel," she says softly. "The evidence of history convinced me. But there are many more prophecies, my friend, many more. And the Word of the Lord through His prophets is *true!*"

She clasps your hand warmly. "Farewell, my friend. We shall meet again one day!" she says as she turns her steps toward the little fishing village.

You will never forget what you have seen here today, and you climb almost reluctantly into the waiting chariot of fire.

"Your next stage on this journey will be to learn about the Word of the Lord through the prophet Nahum, says the steed. "Here is your choice: I may take you to Nahum's village, where you may hear his prophecy against Nineveh; or you may go to Nineveh, to see what kind of city it was more than one hundred years after Jonah preached there. What will you decide?"

Taking the reins in your hands, you make your choice.

If you decide to go to Nahum's village, go to page 48.

If you decide to go to Nineveh (630 B.C.), go to page 69.

(You Have Come to See Petra Today)

The wild cry of a jackal throbs in the still night air and an answering howl echoes from rocky cliffs high above you. A sliver of moon high in the velvet sky sheds little light, and you peer anxiously at your surroundings.

In the faint moonlight you see a huge, desolate building soaring at least thirteen stories high, cut from the rock that towers behind it. *That looks like Petra,* you think, *but what has happened to all the people and animals and traders?* You move your foot and wince in pain as thistles tear into your flesh. You see the gleam of an animal's eyes staring at you from the dense shadows of the columned building and think, *This was once a busy place, but now only the wild animals live here!* Suddenly, an unexpected voice sounds in your ear and you bite your lip to keep from screaming.

"Come along now," murmurs the voice which seems to float out of nowhere. "I have the donkeys loaded. I've stayed too late again, I'm afraid!"

The voice is soothing and comfortable, and you jump only a little as a white face looms out of the shadows. Beneath wispy grey hair, you see the wrinkled face of a man wearing twentieth-century clothes. He smiles cheerfully. "I've always wanted to see Petra at night," he says, sighing contentedly. "What a sight!"

You look uncomfortably at the enormous, empty buildings reaching into the night sky. Towering cliffs on all sides frown down at you, and you

shudder as another jackal wails eerily.

You tumble into the man as he comes suddenly to a stop. Turning to place his hands on your shoulders, he gazes earnestly into your face. "Have you ever listened to the prophecies against Edom?" he asks sharply.

You shake your head in bewilderment, and he rushes into speech again. "Oh, this will never do!" he clucks, diving into the saddlebag on the donkey beside him. "No one should stand in the capital city of ancient Edom and not listen to the prophecies! Even if you've read them a hundred times before, you've never *really* heard them until you listen to them here!" He flings his arm in the general direction of the massive buildings.

With a satisfied cry, the man hauls a well-worn Bible from the saddlebag. "Now, youngster! Sit yourself down right there!" he commands, as he points to a nearby boulder. Removing a small flashlight from a huge pocket, he rustles quickly through the pages. "A-ha!" he says happily, "Here we are, Isaiah 34:10-14. Listen to the Word of the Lord through the prophet Isaiah!"

He settles his dusty glasses firmly on his nose, and begins to read. "From generation to generation it will lie desolate; no one will ever pass through it again. The desert owl and screech owl will possess it.... Her nobles will have nothing there to be called a kingdom... thorns will overrun her citadels, nettles and brambles her strongholds. She will become a haunt for jackals. Desert creatures will meet with hyenas, and wild goats will bleat to each other; there the night creatures will also repose and find for themselves places of rest."

The dim beam of his flashlight makes a tiny point of light in the overpowering vastness of the long-abandoned city. You shiver as you realize that this is most truly a place of desolation, and the blood trickling down your leg is proof of the nettles and thistles! The wild howl of the jackal echoes again in the distance as you ask slowly, "But the prophecy says that no one will ever pass through it, but we're passing through it now!"

A comfortable chuckle shakes your companion's shoulders. "Trade, my friend, trade! This ancient city was on a well-traveled trade route, and believe me, no one passes through here anymore for *that*! The prophecy meant that it would not be on the trade route ever again."

"You mentioned other prophecies?" you question eagerly.

"Oh yes," he nods vigorously. "Isaiah, Jeremiah, Joel, Ezekiel, Amos, and Obadiah *all* prophesied against Edom! Listen!" he commands urgently, flipping the pages in his Bible, "This prophecy is recorded in Ezekiel 25:13, 'Therefore, this is what the Sovereign Lord says: "I will stretch out my hand against Edom and kill its men and their animals. I will lay it waste, and from Teman even to Dedan they will fall by the sword."' Now," he continues triumphantly, "do you know that Teman is today called Ma'an, and is on the very eastern border of ancient Edom? Nothing but desolation lies between Petra and Teman! The Lord has literally laid Edom to waste, as He vowed through His prophet Ezekiel!"

The man grins broadly, and places his Bible back into the saddlebag. Pure white flames blot him from sight as you find yourself back in the chariot.

"I shall take you back to the time of Isaiah once again," chimes the voice. "Here is your decision. You may learn of Isaiah's prediction *by name* of the Persian king who would issue the decree allowing the Hebrews to return to their land from captivity in Babylon."

"But wait," you say haltingly. "That wasn't too hard to do, was it? I mean, wouldn't Isaiah have known who was king of Persia?"

Bell-like chimes fill the air. "No, little one, not then. The children of Israel weren't even captured by Babylon when Isaiah made the prediction. Nor would he know that Babylon would later fall to the Medes and the Persians. So how could he—or any human--know who would be king of Persia more than one hundred and fifty years in the future?

"Your other choice," continues the voice, "is to go to Jerusalem where Isaiah has news for King Hezekiah. Which destination shall you choose?"

Still marveling over what you have seen and heard here in Petra, you take the reins in hand and make your choice.

If you decide to hear Isaiah's prediction, go to page 55.

If you decide to see Isaiah and Hezekiah, go to page 37.